Roses

for
Northern California

Muriel Humenick
Laura Peters

Lone Pine Publishing

© Lone Pine Publishing International Inc.
First printed in 2007   10 9 8 7 6 5 4 3 2 1
Printed in China

Distributed by Lone Pine Publishing
1808 B Street NW, Suite 140
Auburn, WA USA 98001

Website: www.lonepinepublishing.com

Library and Archives Canada Cataloguing in Publication

Includes index.
ISBN-13: 978-1-55105-267-0

1. Rose culture--California, Northern. 2. Roses--California, Northern.
I. Peters, Laura, 1968- II. Title.

SB411.M35 2005   635.9'33734'09794   C2004-904760-4

Illustrations: Ian Dawe
Scanning & Digital Film: Elite Lithographers Co.

Photography: All photographs by Tamara Eder or Robert Ritchie except AARS-2003 22b, 209a, 218b, 234a; Amity Heritage Roses 164b; Rich Baer 59, 183a&b, 193a&b; Bailey Nursery Roses 128a, 167; Paul Barden 43,108, 138, 253; Bridges Roses 70, 72, 243a&b, 250, 255; Conard-Pyle Roses 91a, 111, 128b, 157b, 159b, 171, 192b, 226a, 234b, 235b; David Austin Roses 4, 92c,119, 142a, 146; Saxon Holt 49b, 64, 174a&b, 175a, 247a, 257a; Jackson &Perkins 32, 49a, 55, 150a&b, 155, 159a, 166a, 171a&b, 186, 199a, 208, 209b, 211, 218a, 220, 229a, 240, 249; Brad Jalbert 1, 6a, 215a&b, 241, 244a&b, 246b, 251a&b; J.C. Bakker & Sons 181, 192a; Liz Klose 36a, 68a, 69; Charles W. Lentz 82, 97, 99; George Mander 246a&c; Tim Matheson 33a, 74, 79; Ralph Moore 154a; Kim O'Leary 16b, 27, 50, 85b, 179a, Laura Peters 34 (all) 39b, 40, 41 (all); Pickering Nurseries 30, 109, 114; Reiner Richter 98; Henrique Rodrigues 154b; Rogers Roses 57, 151a&b, 229b, 256a&b; Gene Sasse-Weeks Roses 6b, 140, 158, 170b, 171 179b, 180, 182b, 197, 198, 199b, 201, 205, 206, 213b, 214b, 225, 226b; Weeks Roses 184a&b, 190, 202a&b, 207, 245a&b, 260a&b, 261a&b; Don Williamson 31, 85a.

Front and back cover photographs by Tamara Eder and Robert Ritchie.

PC: P13

CONTENTS

ACKNOWLEDGMENTS 4

INTRODUCTION 5

   Hardiness Zones Map 8

ROSES IN HISTORY 10

ANATOMY & ROSE TERMINOLOGY 14

ROSES IN THE GARDEN 16

   Landscape Uses 16

   Rose Features 18

GETTING STARTED 27

   Climate and Microclimate 27

   Sun 28

   Wind 28

   Competition 28

   Soil 29

BUYING ROSES 31

   Grafted Plants 32

   Own-root Plants 33

   What to Look For 33

PLANTING ROSES 34

   Preparing the Soil 34

   When to Plant 35

   Preparing the Rose 35

   Preparing the Hole 37

   Placing the Rose 38

   Backfill 40

   Peat Cone Theory 42

   Protecting the Rose 43

Transplanting 43

Planting Methods for Different
Landscape Uses 44

CARING FOR ROSES 50

   Watering 50

   Mulching 52

   Fertilizing 53

   Pruning 58

   Removing Rootstock Suckers 67

   Deadheading 68

PROPAGATION 70

PROBLEMS & PESTS 72

   Glossary of Pests & Diseases 78

   Other Problems 87

Rose Lists 90

ABOUT THIS GUIDE 94

THE ROSES 95

RESOURCES 262

GLOSSARY 266

INDEX 268

Acknowledgments

We gratefully acknowledge all who were involved in this project. Thanks to the state and municipal rose societies and gardening clubs for their sound advice and direction. We appreciate the work of the primary photographers, Tamara Eder and Robert Ritchie, as well as entomologist and rosarian Baldo Villegas. Thanks to the many beautiful public and private gardens and garden centers that provided the setting for photographs in this book. Special thanks are extended to the following: American Rose Society, David Austin Roses Ltd., Bridges Roses, Paul Barden, Jackson & Perkins, RogersRoses.com, HelpMeFind.com, Bill Legrice Roses, Weeks Roses, Henrique Rodriguez, Rich Baer, and all others who graciously lent us images for this book.

I would like to thank my parents, Gary and Lucy Peters, for their love and support, and my friends for their endless encouragement. Thanks to the entire Lone Pine team and to the growers and breeders, rosarians, gardeners and garden centers who shared their knowledge with me. –Laura Peters

INTRODUCTION

Among the most beautiful plants to grow, roses reward the gardener in many ways. Thought by many to be demanding and difficult, roses can in fact grow almost anywhere with the right combination of sun, water and care. This book showcases 144 of the best roses for Northern California gardens and contains all the information you need to get growing.

Both ecologically and climatically, Northern California is one of the most diverse regions of the United States. Twelve temperature zones, defined by USDA, can be found here. The temperate climate varies so much because of the diverse topography and the influence of the Pacific Ocean. The most important elements of Northern California's climate are precipitation and temperature. Other factors that affect climate throughout the state include elevation, latitude, airflow and whether a location is coastal or inland. Garden conditions can be adapted to meet roses' requirements. Soil can be made lighter or heavier; exposure to wind can be increased or decreased by careful plant placement; soil fertility or pH can be altered; inadequate rainfall can be

mitigated by irrigation; excess rainfall can be partially compensated for by improved drainage. Roses that are tender for a region can be protected with mulch.

A long coastline and two extensive mountain ranges not only make Northern California beautiful but provide moderating influences that make the climate perfect for growing a vast variety of roses. Coastal regions can offer summer temperatures of 65°–80° F during the day, cooling to 55°–60° F overnight. Temperatures often spike to 100° F two or three times from mid-June through August, and cool to 70° F at night. Humidity in the state is not usually a problem except where summer fog persists daily. Areas with cool summers and persistent fog can be problematic for disease-prone rose varieties, resulting in mildew, rust and blackspot. Reduce the potential for such problems simply by practicing good rose-growing techniques.

Roses grow vigorously in areas with hot summers. Rose varieties

Easy Going (above); Blueberry Hill (below)

with 30 or fewer petals may go from bud to flat-open blossom in a matter of hours while those with more than 30 petals take longer to open but remain open for longer periods. Flower production can be adversely affected during intensely hot weather as plants approach dormancy and stop producing flowers. The flowers produced may be smaller in the intense heat or they may become potpourri right on the plant. Fortunately there are simple methods of preventing this: provide midday or afternoon shade and choose varieties that tolerate heat and stress.

Winter conditions vary widely across Northern California. In general, the interior valleys receive fairly consistent rain. The temperatures in the interior valleys are cold enough to provide ample dormancy for roses to set flowers for the following spring. However, the moderate climate of coastal regions does not. No matter how challenging the site, there are roses that will flourish and provide the gardener with an almost limitless selection of colors, sizes and forms. The versatility of roses, along with their beauty and performance, lies at the root of the continued and growing popularity of the queen of all flowers.

There is more to consider when growing roses in Northern California than climate. The great diversity in soil types and growing conditions is a lesson in the state's varied geology. The coast and western mountain range create ideal conditions for a variety of gardens. The soil itself may

Madame Hardy

Altissimo

Hardiness Zones Map

Minimum Annual Temperature

Zone	Temp (°F)
	-20 to -25
5a	-15 to -20
5b	-10 to -15
6a	-5 to -10
6b	0 to -5
7a	5 to 0
7b	10 to 5
8a	15 to 10
8b	20 to 15
9a	25 to 20
9b	30 to 25
10a	35 to 30

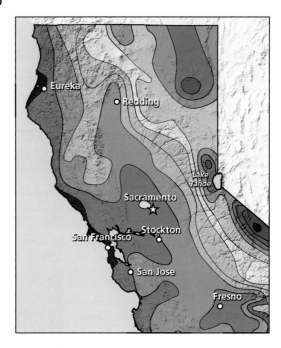

consist of clay, sand or rock and is mostly alkaline. In contrast, gardeners living in the interior valleys will deal with alluvial soils rich in nutrients and a neutral to slightly acidic pH. Covered with fertile river valleys and floodplains, Northern California provides one of the most interesting, challenging and rewarding places to create a rose garden.

The Northern California gardener is supported by an active and hospitable gardening population. Outstanding rose shows, public gardens, show gardens and arboretums throughout the state attract gardeners and growers and are sources of inspiration as well as information. The roses on display are usually well labeled with the information you'll need to cultivate them.

Local rose societies are a wealth of information and inspiration for all rose gardeners, from the beginner to the enthusiast and the rosarian. Many Northern California gardeners have a detailed knowledge of planting and propagation methods, skill in identifying specific roses and plenty of passionate opinions on what works best for any given patch of soil (see Resources, p. 262).

Open yourself to the possibilities and you will be surprised by the

Iceberg

diversity of roses that thrive in Northern California's varied climates. Don't be afraid to try something different or new. Gardening with roses is fun and can be a great adventure if you're willing to take up the challenge. Remember, the rose that best suits its location and purpose will show the least resistance and the best success. Sometimes the rose world can seem daunting, with the overwhelming quantity of potential diseases and pest problems, but rarely will you ever experience more than one or two problems at one time. If all else fails, try, try again, but remember that gardening is discovery, and without discovery there would be little beauty.

A person with a wealth of knowledge and experience and a passionate love for roses is often called a rosarian.

Minnie Pearl

Roses in History

Northern California rose gardeners are part of a long history of rose growers and enthusiasts. Fossil evidence suggests roses flourished up to 32 million years ago; people have been cultivating roses for about 5000 years. Three roses—the gallica, alba and damask—are among the most ancient cultivated plants grown today.

The ancient Romans used rose petals for medicine, perfume, garlands and wedding confetti. Roses were even consumed in puddings and desserts. Roman nobility sponsored large public rose gardens. Cleopatra covered the floors of her palace in a deep layer of fresh rose petals, and the sails of her barge were soaked in rose water. Rose water also flowed through the emperor's fountains, and pillows were stuffed with petals.

The use of rose oil—which today can be found in cosmetics, perfumes and aromatherapy products—originated in ancient Persia. When it was discovered that rose water lasted indefinitely once bottled, people no longer had to surround themselves with bushels of roses for the wonderful fragrance; they merely had to open a bottle of rose water or the pure essential oil, which is also known as attar of roses.

William Lobb

Early Christians associated roses with pagan rites and Roman excesses. Any personal indulgence was considered sinful—including the ancient Roman practice of bathing in water scented with rose oil—and roses fell out of favor. Nevertheless, during the 6th century, St. Benedict planted a little rose garden, or Roseta, which became the model for monastic rose gardens through the Middle Ages. If not for the monastic gardens, some of the ancient roses might have died out.

In the 17th century, roses and rose water were in such demand that they could be used as legal tender to barter or make payments. In France, Napoleon transported gallons of violet and rose scents on his campaigns. It is said that during the Napoleonic Wars, ships carrying roses for Empress Josephine were given free and safe passage. Josephine's rose garden, created in

Charles de Mills

Emperor Nero had a party room with a painted ceiling resembling the heavens, which opened up, sprinkling perfume and flowers on the guests. At one such party, guests were said to have been smothered to death by the enormous quantity of rose petals that fell from the heavens.

Reine des Violettes

The ancient Greeks considered rose water more valuable than its weight in gold. The Roman Catholic Church used rose petals to make the beads for rosaries, hence the name.

the late 18th century at Malmaison, contained every rose known to exist at that time.

The Victorians of the late 19th century were charmed by the rose, and roses began to appear in poetry and prose, representing virtue and innocence. The form of the modern rose garden, with its well-spaced plants and symmetrical form, arose in the 19th century.

Roses decorated the crests of kings and princes in the 15th-century 'Wars of the Roses' between rivals for the English throne. The white rose symbolized the House of York, and the red rose symbolized the House of Lancaster.

Stanwell Perpetual

A formal rose garden

The magnificent beauty of roses continues to inspire poetry, paintings and fragrances. Roses are still bred at an astonishing rate, with over 20,000 cultivated varieties in existence. It's hard to imagine a day without roses, without the sweet fragrance and beauty, medicinal and practical uses and for all they represent. Roses are a wonderful part of our history and will no doubt always be a part of our future.

William Lobb

Carefree Wonder

Tournament of Roses

A Greek legend attributes the creation of the rose to Flora, the goddess of spring and flowers. She found the lifeless body of one of her beautiful nymphs in the forest and asked the gods to give the creature new life by transforming her into a flower, one that surpassed all others in beauty. The request was granted, and the new flower was named Rose, Queen of Flowers.

Anatomy & Rose Terminology

Getting to know the parts and names associated with the rose is a good place for the beginner to start. With a little practice you'll be speaking like a seasoned rosarian.

petal

bud

bract

sepals

true leaf (composed of five or more leaflets)

hip (seedpod)

bud eye

stem

lateral branch

stipule

leaflet

prickles (thorns)

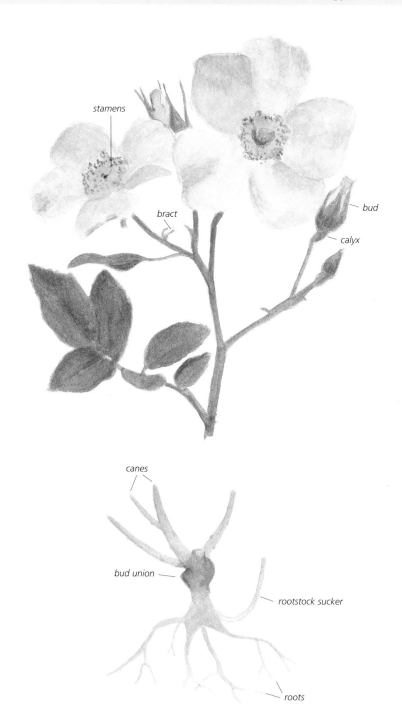

stamens

bract

bud

calyx

canes

bud union

rootstock sucker

roots

Grafted Rose

Roses in the Garden

LANDSCAPE USES

Woody plants—trees and shrubs—are the foundation of your landscape. Roses are flowering shrubs and can be used in any situation that calls for a shrub. Roses can even substitute for annuals and perennials in planting beds. Choose a rose that will work well in the situation you want to use it in. When choosing a rose for a certain purpose or location, consider its cold and heat hardiness, disease resistance, height and spread, maintenance requirements, growth habit, flowering form and color. The following are landscape situations in which roses can be used to good effect.

Beds

Rose beds can be either formal or informal. Formal rose beds are laid out in precise, geometric patterns that allow the maximum number of rose plants to fit in the beds. Roses are chosen for their upright growth habit and uniform height. Variation in height is added by using standard, or tree, roses. Formal rose beds are suitable for large gardens and cut-flower gardens. Formal gardens may also use roses as accents or features rather than devoting the entire beds to them. A drawback to this style of planting is the increased potential for pest and disease outbreaks owing to the roses' close proximity.

Informal rose beds have no precise layout and often include other plants. The choice of which rose to use is limited only by your imagination. Informal style is good for border plantings. Planting roses, or any plants, in odd numbers will help create an informal, natural character.

Tournament of Roses

Berkeley Rose Garden

Hedges

Roses can be grown for informal (non-manicured) hedges using one or two rows of plants. Hedges with two rows often have a staggered arrangement. Species and shrub roses, especially those that sucker, make good rose hedges. The suckers make the hedge thicker from the bottom up. Rose hedges make excellent barriers as they are nearly impenetrable once established. Do not plan to have a highly manicured rose hedge, as few roses respond well to being sheared. Roses such as Linda Campbell and Simplicity, however, do not resent shearing.

Informal planting in mixed bed

Groundcovers

If you have areas that need some color but are hard to plant or maintain, try low-growing or trailing roses. Trailing roses make the best groundcovers. They look good draped over retaining walls or steep slopes. Roses with dense growth can be effective for weed suppression. Begin with an area that is free of weeds for the best result.

Hedge

Covering and masking

Climbing, rambling and larger shrub roses can be used to cover structures such as pergolas, archways, fences, arbors, posts and buildings. Climbers and ramblers require a supporting structure solid enough to handle the weight of their flower-laden canes. It is best to choose a structure that won't require any maintenance, such as painting, over time because it can be tedious to unwind

Groundcover

Handel trained on a trellis

Lavaglut

Gourmet Popcorn

and detach the canes from the support, then reattach the canes again.

Accents
Beautiful roses, with their bright colors and wonderful fragrance, are useful accent plants, drawing attention to themselves and away from less attractive parts of your garden.

Containers
Roses grown in containers, such as planters and hanging baskets, can be used on a deck or balcony or in the garden. They bring the flowers and fragrance close to outdoor sitting areas where they can be enjoyed, and they are a good choice if space is limited. Miniature, polyantha and floribunda roses work well in containers. Standard or tree roses are often grown in containers with shallow-rooted bedding plants. Containers can be used anywhere the growing conditions are right for good rose performance. Containers can be moved to a sunny position and moved again for winter storage.

ROSE FEATURES
Before you go out rose shopping, familiarize yourself with some of the different features and classes of roses. This book is divided into nine sections according to rose classification. Each section begins with an explanation of the characteristics of the class. The sections are species, old garden, modern shrub, groundcover, climbers and ramblers, hybrid tea, floribunda, grandiflora and miniature.

Classification

Classifying roses is complex considering there are approximately 150 species and over 20,000 varieties and cultivars. Classification is becoming more difficult as rose hybridizing continues and hybridizers select breeding parents from a large number of possible candidates. Different groups of rosarians have tried to develop systems of classification that encompass all roses. The American Rose Society (ARS) recognizes 55 official classes, the British Association Representing Breeders recognizes 30 official classes and the World Federation of Rose Societies recognizes 39 official classes. In 1971, delegates to the World Rose Convention adopted a system that divides all roses into climbing and non-climbing classes and then further divides them into recurrent and non-recurrent bloomers.

Adding to the complexity is that different groups classify roses for different purposes. Scientists classify roses according to the botanical characteristics of the flower and plant. The ARS classification system is most useful to those who exhibit their roses in competitions. Nurseries and garden centers classify roses according to their growth habit and use in the landscape, a classification system most practical for the average rose gardener.

Rose societies around the world unite rose growers and disseminate information. Some of the most well-known include:

AHS   American Horticultural Society
ARS   American Rose Society
RNRS Royal National Rose Society
RHS   Royal Horticultural Society

The fragrant Double Delight

Abraham Darby

Evelyn

Fragrance

One of the most important features of roses is the fragrance. The smell of a rose can reach you long before you see the plant. The fragrances can be sweet, spicy, fruity, musky or one of many other wonderful aromas. The petals usually produce the scent, but the leaves, stems and thorns may also be fragrant. In moss roses, the fragrance comes from hairs that cover the stems and calyxes of the flowers.

Many of the modern varieties, such as hybrid teas and floribundas, have little or no scent at all. It is difficult to retain the scent in the hybridizing process. On the other hand, some of the most intense scents come from the modern varieties. Double Delight and Fragrant Cloud, for example, combine superb flower form and color with a strong fragrance. The English roses bred by David Austin Roses Ltd. (also known as Austin roses) combine rich, heady scents of the once-blooming antique and old garden roses with the repeat blooming of the modern varieties.

It is said that double flowers have more fragrance than single flowers, and darker flowers are more fragrant than lighter ones. According to Tom Carruth, hybridizer and director of research at Weeks Roses, these statements are simply not true, and he points to examples of two of his roses as proof. Both Stainless Steel and Memorial Day are light in color and intensely fragrant. The fragrance is strongest, however, on bright, warm, sunny days when the air is a little humid and the wind is light. The aroma is reduced on cloudy days and close to undetectable on rainy days. The best time to enjoy the aroma is when the blooms are just opening in the early morning, which is when roses are picked for the perfume industry.

Some of the older classes of roses such as damasks, gallicas and bourbons have rich, complex aromas and are worthy of growing for this reason alone. If you want a fragrant rose, a good choice would be any of those listed below.

Most Fragrant Roses

- Almost every English rose
- Blanc Double de Coubert
- Double Delight
- Electron
- Fragrant Cloud
- Hansa
- Iceberg
- Lavender Lassie
- Melody Parfumée
- Outta the Blue
- Purple Heart
- *Rosa virginiana*
- Royal Sunset
- Scentimental
- Sheila's Perfume
- Sunsprite

Color

Flower color is the feature most people look for when buying and growing roses. Red, pink, yellow, orange, white, mauve, tan and apricot are a few of the colors available, and there is considerable range within each color. For example, pink

Blanc Double de Coubert

Betty Boop

Double Delight petals can change to red over time

roses range from light pastel pink to deep pink to vivid neon pink. Flowers can show blends of color including different shades of the

Gamble Fragrance Award Winners
- Angel Face
- Chrysler Imperial
- Crimson Glory
- Double Delight
- Fragrant Cloud
- Fragrant Hour
- Granada
- Mister Lincoln
- Papa Meilland
- Secret
- Sunsprite
- Sutter's Gold
- Tiffany

Playboy

The Gamble Fragrance Award is a prestigious award given to a rose that exhibits a good, strong fragrance but also has vigor, good pest and disease resistance, good color and is a top seller for more than five years. To date there have been only 11 winners of this award, and these varieties are readily available.

same color or two different colors on the same flower—often referred to as a bicolored or multi-colored flower. Roses come in almost every color except black, blue and green. There are roses that look black but are really deep red. The green-flowered rose, *Rosa chinensis viridiflora,* has no true petals. The green petal-like sepals give the flower its color.

Flower color is affected by sunlight, temperature, soil and water. In the absence of heat, dark-colored flowers may appear muddy rather than vibrant while pastel colors are usually clear and attractive. Some colors fade readily and others are prone to sunburn. If your rose has the right environmental conditions and is healthy, you will almost be guaranteed gorgeous blooms.

The International Registration Authority for Roses, run by the ARS, authorizes 18 official colors for all roses. Every new rose variety registered has to list one of the 18 official colors as its color. The color descriptions in catalogs and some reference books (including this one) are generally more detailed than the official color listing.

Flower forms

There are a variety of rose flower forms. One of the most familiar is

Whisper

the pointed hybrid tea flower, the classic rose shape we have come to expect when we give or receive roses. Other forms include the flat, single flowers of some species roses and the quartered rosette flowers of some of the old garden roses.

The terms *single, semi-double* and *double* refer to the number of individual petals and their arrangement on the flower. Single flowers are arranged in a single row with no less than five and up to twelve petals. Semi-double flowers have 13 to 20 petals arranged in two or three rows. Double flowers have 20 or more petals. Some sources have an additional category for flowers with 35 or more petals. These are called *very double* or *fully double* flowers.

The following are the different rose flower forms:
Flat: Open flowers that are single or semi-double with the petals perpendicular to the stem.
Cupped: Open flowers that are single or semi-double with petals that curve upward forming a shallow cup.
Pointed: Semi-double to double flowers with high-pointed centers created by the tight wrap of petals before they fully unfurl. One of the most familiar forms.
Urn shaped: Semi-double to double flowers with flat tops and slightly outward curving petals. Similar to the pointed shape but appears slightly looser and more open in the center.

Flat form

Cupped form

Pointed form

Urn-shaped form

Rounded form

Rosette form

Quartered rosette form

Pompom form

Rounded: Double flowers with overlapping petals of even size, creating a rounded bowl silhouette.

Rosette: Double flowers with slightly overlapping, confused, unevenly sized petals creating a flattish outline.

Quartered Rosette: Double flowers with petals of uneven size forming a quartered appearance and a flattish outline.

Pompom: Double flowers with many small petals forming a small, rounded outline.

Substance

Substance is the amount of moisture in the petals, which affects the texture, firmness, thickness, stability and durability of the petals. Roses have substance at different levels, and rose flowers with substance have a long vase life.

Hips

Hips are the fruits of roses, and are produced when flowers are pollinated by bees and left to ripen. Hips can provide fall and winter color. Most ripen to shades of red, orange and yellow and come in a variety of shapes, from round and globe-like to football shaped to teardrop shaped.

The formation of hips and production of seeds in the hips signal the plant to stop flowering and prepare for winter dormancy. Not all roses produce hips. In the wild, birds and other animals feed on ripe hips.

Hardiness

The hardiness of a plant is its ability to withstand climatic and other environmental conditions. Cold hardiness designates the plant's ability to survive the minimum average cold temperatures for an area. There are 15 zones in the newly revised USDA hardiness map, each of which represents a 10° F difference in average annual minimum temperature. Lower numbered zones represent areas with the coldest winter temperatures, and higher numbered zones represent areas with warmer winter temperatures. Some classes of roses, such as the rugosa roses, thrive with no winter protection in areas that get quite cold. A rose is said to be tender if it survives winter temperatures no colder than 10°–20° F. Heat hardiness is similarly represented by zones. Each zone indicates the average number of days each year that a given area experiences temperatures over 86° F. That is the point at which plants begin suffering physiological damage from the heat. The zones range from zone 1 (less than one heat day) to zone 12 (more than 210 heat days). Hardiness ratings are general, however. Other factors can affect what can and cannot successfully grow in a particular location based on exposure, winds and shelter. These areas are referred to as microclimates.

Rose hip (seedpod)

Standard rose (tree rose)

Plant form

Plant form is the shape and growth habit of the plant. The forms available today can be easily used in the garden and landscape. Growth can be upright, such as the hybrid teas with their straight, sturdy canes. Roses can also have graceful arching canes or they can be mounding shrubs that rival any of the flowering shrubs used in landscapes. Climbing and rambling roses produce long, supple canes that can be trained on trellises, fences and pillars or left alone to form large, spreading shrubs. Standards, also known as tree roses, have a lollipop look created by budding or grafting a rose plant onto a tall stem. This form is also available in a trailing or spreading form, resulting in an umbrella-like appearance.

Foliage

Rose foliage can be delicate and fern-like with many leaflets per leaf, such as *Rosa pimpinellifolia*, or large and crinkled like the rugosa roses. The leaves can be dull or shiny, in shades of dark green, light green, blue-green and gray-green. Some roses have excellent fall color in shades of yellow, red and bronze-red. *Rosa glauca* (*Rosa rubrifolia*) is a rose with beautiful foliar color, bearing

Rose foliage can vary in texture and color.

blue-green to purple foliage that dramatically contrasts with the pink flowers in season but is most stunning in autumn.

Thorns

What we usually refer to as thorns are really prickles, defined botanically as small, thin, sharp outgrowths of the young bark, whereas thorns are sharp outgrowths from the wood of the stem. Rose prickles come in a variety of sizes and levels of nastiness. The prickles of *Rosa acicularis* (the Prickly Rose) are thin and sharp and cover the stems. The Wingthorn Rose, *Rosa sericea pteracantha*, has large, bright red, winged prickles, which provide color all year. Some roses, such as Thérèse Bugnet, have large, hooked barbs that make pruning a truly dangerous task. Regardless of the type of thorn, handling roses requires care and attention.

Thorns

Getting Started

Roses are not difficult to grow once you consider a few basics. Planning is essential, though. Good planning will allow you to plant the right rose in the right location for long-term success. Complete a site analysis, which can be as simple as walking around your garden and observing the conditions at different times of the day or season, to determine if you have the right environment for growing roses. You might find it helpful to make an overhead-view scale drawing of your property to plan the layout of your garden.

CLIMATE AND MICROCLIMATE

Climatic conditions to consider before selecting a rose include the temperature range of your area, the risk and timing of frost, prevailing winds and the amount of rainfall, humidity and sunshine available. It is far easier to select a rose that is adapted to your local climate than to battle against the climate. Most roses will grow in a range of hardiness zones, with minimum winter temperature being the most limiting factor. Zones should be used only as guidelines. With adequate winter protection, some tender roses may be grown in zones colder than they are rated. Check the hardiness zones map on page 8 for a general guide to hardiness zones in Northern California.

A microclimate is an area that has a slightly different climate than the surrounding area. The area to the south side of a building will be warmer than other areas of a yard. The area under the eaves of the house will be drier than other parts of a yard. The top of a hill or slope will be drier than the bottom. Cold air runs downhill, so the bottom of the slope will be cooler than the top. Part of your site analysis will be to determine the microclimates in your yard. Warm microclimates enable the gardener to successfully grow roses that are not completely hardy, with minimal to extra winter protection based on the initial zoning.

Rose garden at Filoli

SUN

Roses require a minimum of six hours of sunlight per day for good flowering. Morning sun is best as it helps the foliage dry quickly, lessening the chance of fungal disease. Any rose grown in full shade will be weak and spindly with very few to no flowers. Some roses, such as the hybrid musks, are better adapted to growing in light to partial shade. If your garden gets intensely hot in summer, some light afternoon shade will help prevent sun damage to the flowers and foliage. In fact, lavender-colored roses prefer afternoon shade in hot valley areas.

Blanc Double de Coubert

Nicole

WIND

Wind can be the enemy of roses, increasing evaporation from the soil and drying a rose out quickly, especially when there has been little rain. A strong wind can dry and shred flowers. Winter wind can dry and destroy canes. Shelter your roses from the prevailing winds with fences, buildings and hedges.

Some wind, however, can help roses. A gentle breeze helps keep foliage dry, minimizing the incidence of disease. That breeze can also carry the fragrance of a rose a long way.

COMPETITION

Roses are heavy feeders and drinkers. They expend a great deal of energy producing their flowers and don't like to share root space with many other plants. Trees, turf, weeds and other garden plants may compete with roses for space and resources. In particular, avoid planting roses near trees such as weeping willow, mulberry, spruce and ash, which have large, wide-spreading root systems. Plants with shallow, well-behaved root systems are good companions for roses.

SOIL

Soil provides support for the plant, holds and provides nutrients and water and makes oxygen available to the roots. Roses prefer a fertile, well-drained, moisture-holding loam with at least five percent organic matter, but they can grow in a wide range of soil types.

Testing a location's drainage

Soil is made up of particles of different sizes. Clay particles are very small or fine, silt particles are slightly larger but still considered fine, and sand particles are the largest of the three. Soils with a high percentage of clay particles are considered heavy, while soils with a high percentage of sand particles are considered light. Heavy soils hold water and nutrients but they do not drain well. Loams are soils with a balanced mix of clay, silt and sand particles. Roses like loams and clay-based soils as long as there is adequate drainage. Sandy soils require more frequent watering and fertilizing.

It is important to consider the pH level (the scale on which acidity or alkalinity is measured) of soil, which influences the availability of nutrients. An acid soil has a pH under 7.0 while an alkaline soil has a pH over 7.0. Roses perform best in slightly acidic soils, with a pH between 6.0 and 7.0. Soil pH can be changed but it

takes a long time and routine applications of either sulfur or lime to maintain the desired level. It is a good idea to check the pH of your soil at least every two years.

Soil Testing

Complete soil testing kits are available from private or government labs. A complete soil test will tell you the pH; the percentage of sand, silt, clay and organic matter; the amount and type of nutrients available and the degree of salinity. This information helps you plan your fertilizing

Buff Beauty

program, and laboratories usually provide recommendations for correcting soil deficiencies (See soil testing resources p. 264).

Garden centers sell simple test kits for pH and some major nutrients. Based on the results of the test, the garden center staff should be able to make recommendations about which amendments to use and how to use them. Soil amendments are used to improve fertility, drainage and workability. Read about amendments in the Planting Roses section of this introduction.

It may also be a good idea to have your water tested, especially if you are using well water. Knowing the

pH, mineral composition and salt content of your water source can help identify problems. Some nutrients can be rendered unavailable to plants depending on the mineral content of your water.

Drainage

Roses use a lot of water but do not like to have their roots sitting in water. The soil must drain well enough to allow air to reach the roots and hold enough water for the rose to use. Drainage of heavy soils can be improved by adding organic matter or gypsum, by installing perforated drainage tile under the roses, double digging (see p. 34) or by using raised beds. Sandy soils drain water quickly but do not retain nutrients for long. Organic matter helps sandy soils hold more water and nutrients.

If you are unsure that the spot you have chosen will drain well enough to prevent standing water, try this simple test. Dig a test hole 12" wide and deep. Fill the hole to the top with water and let it drain completely. Fill the hole with water again and note the time it takes for the water to completely drain from the hole. A drainage rate of $1/2$" or less per hour is considered poor and will limit plant selection or require expensive drainage work to alleviate the problem.

Harison's Yellow

Buying Roses

Roses can be purchased from nurseries, garden centers, mail-order suppliers, supermarkets and department stores. You will likely get the best quality plants and advice from nurseries, garden centers and suppliers that specialize in roses. Roses produced locally are good choices because they are already adapted to the climate. Ordering roses through the mail or over the Internet is very convenient and the roses come right to your door. (Refer to resource list, p. 262).

Roses are available for sale in three ways: bare-root, packaged bare-root and containerized (in pots).

Some roses come bare-root, especially from mail-order nurseries. These roses are dug up from the field when they are dormant. The soil is removed from the roots and the roots are wrapped in plastic, newspaper or wood wool before shipping. Ideally the roses should arrive in the dormant state with no new growth. The roses sometimes start growing during transport. Before planting, remove any shoots longer than 2".

Packaged bare-root roses are often found in supermarkets and department stores. Each rose comes in a plastic or waxed cardboard container with the roots surrounded by moist sawdust, peat moss, wood chips or shredded paper. Buy packaged roses early in the season when the roses are still relatively dormant. Even if you can't plant them right away, you can store them in a cool location. The

canes of packaged roses are usually waxed to prevent them from drying out during shipping and before planting. The wax would normally come off during the growing season but because of the heat in Northern California, especially in the valley, the wax can actually burn the canes long before it naturally wears off. Roses with waxed canes are not recommended for use in Northern California. Container roses are grown in pots, not fields, though some stock sold in containers may have been bare-root plants potted by the nursery staff. Own-root roses (see p. 33) are commonly available as container stock. Container roses are available for sale throughout the growing season and can be planted any time. Often a container rose will be in flower and you can see exactly what you are purchasing.

GRAFTED PLANTS

Today, most roses are bud-grafted, a process in which a bud eye from a selected variety is grafted onto the rootstock. When the bud starts to grow, the top of the rootstock plant is removed. The energy that would have been used by the top is all directed towards the newly grafted bud. The area where the new bud is grafted onto the rootstock is called the bud union.

Budded plants mature more quickly than plants from cuttings. Some growers claim the flowers from a grafted plant are bigger and better than flowers from the same variety grown on its own roots. At one time it was believed that using a cold-hardy rootstock would increase the cold hardiness of the grafted variety, but in fact only the rootstock remains hardy and its hardiness does not transfer to the variety grafted on top of it.

Growers and hybridizers have many different rootstocks available. Choose a rootstock that will provide the desired characteristics. Always ask the supplier if the rootstock is appropriate for your area. For our area, Dr. Huey is the best rootstock.

Standard roses, often referred to as tree roses, have two grafts and an elongated main stem. The lower graft is between the rootstock and the stem. The other graft is between the stem and the variety at the top. Standard roses do not fit into any specific rose class, because the variety grafted to

Red Ribbons

the top could be a miniature, floribunda or hybrid tea.

Own-root plants

Own-root plants, as the name suggests, are grown on their own roots. They take longer to reach maturity than budded plants and are more expensive to produce but can be very long-lived and are hardier in colder areas than grafted plants. Old garden roses, miniature roses, shrub roses, species roses, ramblers and climbers are often grown on their own roots.

WHAT TO LOOK FOR

When purchasing any rose, make sure the roots are moist. It is easy to check for moist soil if the rose is in a container. It is more difficult, but possible, to examine the roots of packaged roses. If the package is very light or you can see any dry soil or planting mix, the roots are probably dry.

Examine the root system. Bare-root roses should have a mass of long, fibrous roots. Avoid roses that have short spindly roots or that have had their roots pruned. For container roses, ensure that the roots have white tips and are not encircling the inside of the container or growing out the bottom of the container. Avoid plants with blackened or girdled roots. Roses that have weak root systems will have a tough time establishing.

The canes of bare-root and packaged roses should be supple and dark green, have small buds and be at least as thick as a pencil no matter the grade

Root-bound plant

(see sidebar). Avoid plants with dry, dead and shriveled canes. Any visible pith should be white or green. Roses with tan or brown piths may have sustained some damage. Avoid bare-root roses with new growth in the form of long, pale shoots.

Roses are sorted into three grades according to the size and number of main canes. More often than not, you'll come across only Grade 1 or Grade 1 1/2 roses, indicating that the rose you've chosen is of excellent quality. It is best to invest a little more money when purchasing a rose, ensuring that it is of superior quality. Don't settle for cheap roses—the old cliché rings true: you get what you pay for.

Felicia

Planting Roses

Preparing the proper planting site is an investment of time that will be rewarded when your rose blooms well. Proper care, placement and planting are critical to a rose's establishment and long-term success. Preparing the soil is the most important step, and it can begin long before planting.

PREPARING THE SOIL

Based on a soil test (see p. 29 and Resources, p. 264), amend your soil as necessary with organic or inorganic amendments. Especially if you are planting a large area of roses, you should prepare the area the summer prior to winter planting so the soil has a chance to settle over winter before you plant your roses. If the soil settles too much, it is easy to top it up before planting. You can prepare the soil just before planting, but be aware that your rose might settle more deeply than is recommended.

There are many possible methods for preparing an area to plant roses. The following method is referred to as **double digging** and is often used when the planting area is compacted or rocky or in need of being turned and amended. Dig and set aside the topsoil from the planting area. Turn over the subsoil with a garden fork.

Topsoil set aside

Adding amendments to subsoil

Mixing soil and amendments

Adding amendments to topsoil

To accommodate bush roses such as hybrid teas, grandifloras and floribundas, the prepared area should be 18–24" deep and 24" wide for each rose. If you are planting miniatures, the depth and width can be 12". Robust climbers, ramblers and shrub roses may need an area up to 18–24" deep and 4' wide.

Sometimes it is impossible to dig the soil to the desired depth because of rock or hardpan. Raised beds are the best possible solution to provide the necessary soil depth and drainage. If that fails, choose a different location.

Add any amendments and mix them in well, then replace the topsoil.

Organic amendments include compost, well-rotted manure (preferably chicken, horse, rabbit or sheep manure), peat moss, leaf mold, bonemeal, alfalfa pellets and agricultural byproducts such as seed shells and husks, sawdust and composted wood chips. Inorganic amendments include superphosphate, limestone, coarse sand, vermiculite and perlite. The addition of Epsom salts (magnesium sulfate) is discouraged as it can compromise the balance of micronutrients in the soil. Each amendment has different properties and should be added to the soil only if deemed necessary by a soil test.

Use only thoroughly composted materials. Amendments such as fresh manure could burn a rose's roots, and uncomposted organic materials, such as sawdust or woodchips, use the available nitrogen from the soil to aid their decomposition.

A common practice for rose growers is to add 25 to 33 percent of soil volume of compost or well-rotted manure—for example, adding 3–4" of compost or well-rotted manure to soil at a depth of 12".

WHEN TO PLANT

Roses establish best in cool, moist soil. Planting in winter is best, from December to February. Bare-root roses are planted in winter while they're still dormant.

Container roses can be planted anytime except during periods of extreme heat. Container roses are the only roses that can be planted in summer because they already have an established root system. Diligent watering is mandatory for proper establishment of container roses and is even more important for those planted in summer.

Elina

Soaking bare-root roses

PREPARING THE ROSE

All roses should be planted as soon as possible after purchase. Your new rose will require some preparation. If you buy a container rose, the preparation begins at the point of purchase. The rose must be thoroughly saturated before you take it home, so that the roots remain moist during transport. If you are transporting the rose in a car, be aware of the temperature, as excess heat dries plants out. If you are using an open truck for transport, lay the plant down or cover it to protect it from the wind, as even a short trip can be traumatic for a plant. Container roses can be planted days, weeks and even months after purchase, provided that they are kept moist during the wait. Place container roses in the sun but away from drying winds. Container roses dry out quickly, so it may be necessary to water them daily.

If you are going to plant within 24 hours, stand the roses in a bucket of muddy water, ensuring the roots are completely covered with water. Some rosarians soak the entire plant. The mud in the water will lightly coat the roots, helping to prevent desiccation during planting. Soak the plant for 12 to 24 hours but no longer.

If you have to store bare-root roses for a couple of days, do not remove the packaging but open it just enough to check that the roots are moist, adding water if necessary. Close the package and place it in a cool, dry, frost-free area such as a refrigerator or an unheated garage.

If your garden is too muddy to work when your roses arrive, you will need longer storage. The usual

Heeling-in bare-root roses

method is called heeling-in, which involves digging a trench in a well-drained area such as an edge of a vegetable garden or under an eave, preferably with shade. The trench should be 12" deep on one side with the bottom of the trench sloping up at a 45-degree angle. Lay the roses in the trench with the roots toward the bottom of the trench. Cover completely with soil except for the tips of the canes and water the entire trench. Keeping the tips uncovered helps you find the rose later, and the soil covering keeps the roses from drying out.

This method works well as long as the weather remains somewhat cool. If freezing weather is in the forecast, cover the heeled-in roses with mulch or burlap. Some sources say that heeled-in roses can be stored for a few months, but every effort should be made to plant as soon as possible. Use caution when digging up heeled-in roses to avoid damaging the roots and canes. Long-term storage is usually not necessary as mail-order suppliers time their shipments to coincide with the arrival of spring in your area.

PREPARING THE HOLE

In your prepared rose area, you must dig a hole for each rose.

For container stock, the depth in the center of the hole should be equal to the depth of the rootball, and one-and-a-half times the width of the container. Certain classes of roses may need to be planted deeper than others.

Dainty Bess

For bare-root stock, the hole is usually 24" deep and 24" wide, big enough to completely contain the expanded roots with a little extra room on the sides and a cone-shaped central mound (see diagram). The mound helps to evenly space the roots in the hole, prevents the rose from sinking as the soil settles and encourages excess water to drain away from the roots. Some rose growers form the mound in the center of the hole with amended backfill rather than soil alone.

If you are considering using mushroom compost, check with the supplier to ensure the compost has low salt and is pesticide free.

It is a good idea to roughen the sides of the hole with a garden fork or trowel so that it's easier for roots to penetrate out of the hole.

PLACING THE ROSE

Plant your rose on an overcast or rainy day. If that is not possible, try to plant it during the early morning or early evening, when the temperatures are cooler, rather than in the middle of the day.

Bare-root roses

Remove the plastic and sawdust from the roots or retrieve the rose from your temporary storage. Prune out any broken, diseased or rotten roots or canes. Center the plant over the central mound and fan out the roots in the hole.

If your rose is grafted, the position of its bud union depth is important. Plant the bud union approximately 2" above the surface of the soil. This will allow for settling so the bud union doesn't sink too deeply.

Cut the remaining canes of hybrid teas, grandifloras and floribundas to a height of 10–12". Some rosarians cut the canes to 5–8", which causes the new canes to form lower on the plant, giving a much bushier look. Recent research has shown that roses perform better with more foliage. Allowing weaker canes to grow will provide the rose with more foliage and thus more energy in its establishment year. Other than to remove broken or diseased canes, fall-planted container roses should not be cut back until all other roses are cut back for winter.

Container roses

Container roses are very easy to plant. Containers are made of plastic or pressed fiber. Before planting, water the rootball thoroughly and gently remove the container to check

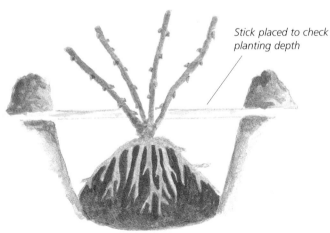

Stick placed to check planting depth

Bare-root stock on central mound

the root mass. If the plant is girdled or root-bound (if the roots circle around the inside of the container between the container and the soil), the roots must be loosened. Any large roots encircling the soil or growing into the center of the root mass instead of outward should be removed before planting. A sharp pair of hand pruners (secateurs) or a pocket knife will work very well for this task. Some roses might not have been in their containers long enough to develop enough roots to allow the container to be removed without soil falling away from the roots. If soil falls away from the roots, the new feeder roots can be damaged, but do not be discouraged. If the soil falls away, plant the rose as you would plant bare-root stock.

All containers must be removed before planting. Although some containers appear to be made of peat moss or natural fibers, they won't be able to decompose as fast as growing roots require. The roots may not be able to penetrate the pot sides and the fiber will wick moisture away from the roots. The roots may never even leave the pot, resulting in girdled, constricted roots.

Place the rose, pot and all, on top of the central mound to check planting depth. Adjust if necessary.

Roses grown on their own roots (old garden roses or species roses) do not have a bud union. The crown should be planted 1" below soil level or at the same level it is in the pot.

Remove the pot and place the root-ball onto the central mound. Prune out any dead or diseased canes.

Miniatures

Most miniature roses are sold as container roses and can be planted the same way as larger container roses. Most miniatures are grown in greenhouses and must be hardened off before planting.

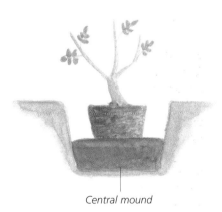

Central mound

Planting a container rose

Checking planting depth

Standard or tree roses

Standard roses usually have two bud unions, although several major rose growers are now producing trees with only one bud union. When planting standard roses, ensure the lower bud union is at the proper depth. Use a sturdy, rot-proof stake long enough to be set into undisturbed soil and reach up to just below the top bud union. The stake can be placed on the sunny side, which helps protect the main stem from sun scald, or to the side of the prevailing wind for extra support. Tie the main stem to the stake about halfway up the stake and near the top. Prune the top as for bare-root plantings.

Root pruning

We do not recommend root pruning when planting or transplanting other than to remove broken, diseased or dead roots for bare-root plantings. Scientific studies have confirmed that root pruning shocks the plant by throwing hormones out of balance. It increases water and nutrient stresses as well as the susceptibility of the rose to insect and disease attacks.

BACKFILL

With the rose in the hole it is time to replace the soil. Container stock will usually stay upright during backfilling while a bare-root rose will need to be held in position.

If you have not already amended the soil in your rose bed, amend the backfill soil. Leaf mold, well-rotted manure, compost, bonemeal and moist peat moss are all suitable amendments.

When backfilling, it is important to have good root-to-soil contact to help the plant's stability and establishment. Large air pockets remaining after backfilling could cause unwanted settling and increase the risk of desiccation. Tamping or stepping down on the backfilled soil used to be recommended, but the risk of injury to the roots and compacting

Backfilling hole

50% backfilled

Adding bonemeal to backfill

Settling backfill with water

Settling backfilled topsoil with water

Planting process complete

Bonemeal is a slow-release fertilizer and will gradually add important nutrients for root development.

of the soil has made this practice fall out of favor. Use water to settle the soil gently around the roots and in the hole, taking care not to drown the plant. Backfill in small amounts bit by bit rather than all at once. Add some soil then water it in, repeating until the hole is full.

Use any soil remaining after backfilling to top up the soil level around the plant after the backfilled soil settles and to mound up around the canes with loose mulch.

Amending the backfill in heavy clay soils will provide a light soil medium for the root system to grow in until the roots reach the heavy clay. Some of the roots will have difficulty penetrating the clay, resulting in what is known as 'flowerpot syndrome,' when the roots grow only in and around the amended soil, as if the rose were grown in a clay flowerpot. To prevent such a problem, remove the heavy subsoil and amend it before backfilling. The best additions are forest humus and gypsum, which break down clay-based soils. If you don't want to amend so extensively, at least score the bottom of the

A salvaged peat pot also works well as a collar to break the plant's dormancy. Simply knock out the bottom of the peat pot and place it around the bush.

planting hole with a garden fork to help the roots break through the heavy soil. Other alternatives include selecting another location or using raised beds.

PEAT CONE THEORY

The following "Peat Cone Theory," courtesy of rosarian Muriel Humenick from El Dorado, CA, can be incorporated when a newly planted bush is seen to be suffering. Cane dieback and shriveling and a lack of new growth are sure signs of decline. Such conditions can occur when the plant's roots are exposed to air for a long time or when the plant is held in cold storage for too long.

If all proper planting methods were incorporated but the plant still shows signs of decline, use the Peat Cone Theory to break the plant's dormancy. This will enable it to draw the moisture it needs from the soil and begin to grow. Place a "collar" made of material such as tar paper strips, metal strips or cardboard around the bush, and fill the inside of the collar with material that stays damp when moistened, like sphagnum moss or peat moss. This inner material should be wet when it's put inside the collar; work the peat moss with your hands to encourage it to soak up water, if necessary.

Remove the collar when you see swelling buds on the canes or leaves developing. Allow the peat moss to fall away gradually and become part of your mulch.

PROTECTING THE NEWLY PLANTED ROSE

Once the rose is in the hole and properly backfilled, mound mulch over it to a depth of 10–12", less if the canes are shorter. If you do not have enough soil, you can use mulch. Mounding the soil helps prevent desiccation of the canes while the rose rebuilds its feeder roots. Ensure the entire mound remains moist.

In three to four weeks, less if the weather is mild, the bud eyes will swell and produce new canes and foliage. When you see the new growth you can slowly remove the mound by gently washing it away. Choose overcast or rainy days for this task. Hot, sunny days will scorch the newly exposed, delicate shoots. It should take about a week to remove the mound, enough time to give the new, tender growth a chance to harden off. If there is a risk of frost, recover the rose with soil or mulch.

If the rose fails to break dormancy, mound with moist peat or mulch and cover with plastic, creating a mini-greenhouse. Check daily to ensure the humidity under the plastic is not causing disease or rot and the peat remains moist but

not soggy. Check for signs of burning as well. Allow new growth to harden off as stated above. If the rose still doesn't break dormancy, cut the canes and look at the pith. If the pith is brown and no white tips are evident on the roots, it's time to dig up the rose and get a replacement.

TRANSPLANTING EXISTING ROSES

Roses are said to dislike being moved once established, but the need may arise. The younger the rose, the more likely it will re-establish successfully when moved to a new location.

If you are moving a rose to a spot where another rose previously grew, add fresh soil or lots of compost, because the previous rose may have depleted the soil of nutrients. If planting a new rose in a spot where a diseased rose was, it is very important to use fresh soil or lots of compost. There may be populations of

When planting container grafted roses, make sure that the bud union is the same depth as that required by bare-root roses.

Magic Carrousel

Staggered double-row hedge

organisms in the old soil, such as soil fungi, viruses and nematodes, that could use the rose as a host plant. This is sometimes referred to as soil sickness. The bad organisms attack the young feeder roots of new roses, severely limiting the rose's ability to absorb water and nutrients. Planting your rose with fresh soil will provide a new source of nutrients and aid in its establishment.

Transplanting roses can be complicated. Pursue information on this topic by consulting a local rose growers' society, which should be able to provide detailed information or direct you to it.

PLANTING METHODS FOR DIFFERENT LANDSCAPE USES AND VARIETIES

Roses can be used for a variety of tasks in the landscape. The following tips will help you as you think about planting roses in specific landscape situations.

Hedges

When planting hedges, staggering the rows will allow the maximum number of roses for the size of the bed or hedge, gives a good mass effect and allows all the roses to be seen from one side. The modern bush roses are often planted in staggered rows, with 30–36" between plants. The more vigorous shrub roses are planted at two-thirds of the spread at maturity so the branches eventually intermingle to form the hedge. For taller hedges, the planting distance can be increased slightly. The best rose hedges are grown from own-root roses because any suckers developing from the roots will help thicken up the hedge and are from the rose variety you planted.

Climbers

Planting climbers requires some extra preparation. Have the support structure in place and a supply of rose ties. Special rose ties are available at your local garden center or from specialty rose nurseries, but rose ties can be any device or piece of non-abrasive material used to tie the rose to the supports. Support can be stiff wires strung horizontally along a wall or hooks attached to a wooden fence. Hooks make rose maintenance and training a little easier because the canes merely have to be set into the hooks rather than tied to a wire. It really doesn't matter what the support is as long as it is sturdy enough to support the weight of the plant in full bloom.

Plant the climber about 18" from the wall, fence or whatever you have chosen to train the climber on. Angle the canes toward the lowest support and tie them in place. You will want the canes to form a fan shape as you attach them to the support.

Leave enough room between the tie and the structure for the cane to grow—your finger should fit easily

Planting tip: Steep willow twigs in water for a week and use the water when settling the backfill soil and when first watering the newly planted rose. The water contains a natural rooting hormone and salicylic acid, which both aid in root regeneration.

into the space. This space will prevent the growing cane from being girdled or strangled.

Groundcovers

When planting roses as a groundcover, you must first remove any weeds. An easy, non-toxic method is to pasteurize the soil:

- Remove any surface weeds and add soil amendments
- Rake the area smooth and cover it with a sheet of flexible, black plastic
- Bury the edges of the plastic and leave in place for a few months
- The heat under the plastic will prevent annual weed seeds, soil diseases and insects from penetrating the soil
- Remove the plastic
- Plant, disturbing the soil as little as possible.

The way you space and plant groundcover roses will depend on what roses you are using. A rule of thumb is to space at two-thirds of the spread at maturity. For consistency

Single-row hedge

and a good massing effect, all the roses should be the same variety. After planting the roses, cover the entire area with mulch, being careful not to mound the mulch directly around the crown of the rose.

Planting in containers

Planting roses in containers is different than planting container roses, which are often meant to be in their pots temporarily. Any rose can be planted in a container, but the larger the rose, the larger the container you will need and the heavier it will be once it is filled with soil. If the containers are too heavy to lift, casters on the bottom of the container can make them easier to move. Containers can be made of many different materials, including wood, plastic, metal or clay. Straight-sided containers offer more room for the roots than those with tapered sides. Ensure the bottom of the container has an adequate number of drainage holes. Choose a container that won't be so heavy that it's difficult to move, especially when full of moist dirt. There are pots made of materials such as fiberglass and plastic resins that look like terracotta or ceramic but are light and last much longer than natural materials.

Smaller containers will require water and fertilizer more often. Choose a container that will accommodate the rootball's growth over a long period of time.

Floribundas, polyanthas, miniatures and the smaller hybrid teas are excellent choices for containers. Miniatures can be in containers as small as 12" in diameter and 10–12" deep. Floribundas, polyanthas and

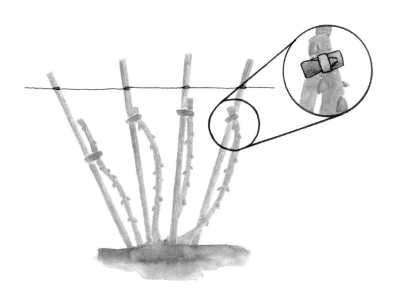

Attaching climber or rambler canes to support

hybrid teas should have pots with a minimum 16" diameter and depth. For standard roses, match the container size to what the variety grafted to the top of the standard needs.

Don't use gravel at the bottom of your container. Studies have shown that the soil on top of the gravel must be completely saturated with water before it drains through the gravel beneath. A fiberglass or metal

Planting roses in containers can be a daunting task in hot areas. Drip irrigation is sometimes the only way to maintain a healthy level of moisture for a container-bound rose in the hot valleys. Growing roses in containers works best, however, on the coast.

Rise 'n' Shine

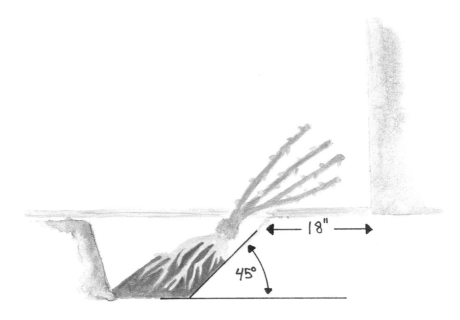

Proper planting distance and angle for climbers and ramblers

Royal Sunset

Cupcake

window screen is better for covering the drainage holes on the bottom of the container; water will drain out but soil will not.

The soil for containers must be non-compacting, moderately rich, moisture retaining and well drained. Sterile planting mixes, some specifically designed for roses, are available from your local nursery or garden center. Sterile mixes won't provide any nutrients to the rose, however, so make sure to supplement with a regular fertilizing program. A good mix is one-third loam, one-third organic matter such as compost or well-rotted manure and one-third coarse sand. When ordering soil, specify loam and not topsoil. To ensure good results, test the pH of any soil you bring into your rose garden. When planted and settled, the soil should be 1–2" below the rim of the container to facilitate a thorough watering without run-off.

Planting in a container is similar to planting in the ground. Place the rose in the container and backfill in the same way you would when planting in the ground.

Plants in containers may need protection from extreme temperatures. Rot-resistant wood such as cedar makes an attractive container that offers protection from excessive heating and cooling. Containers made of other materials may need help keeping the roots cool. One method is to place one container into another with a minimum 1" space between the containers for insulating material such as moistened vermiculite, sawdust or Styrofoam packing peanuts. Alternatively, the inside of a container may be lined with stiff foam insulation for straight-sided containers or a couple of layers of carpet underlay for curved-sided containers.

Every 3 to 4 years, a container rose needs to be removed, root pruned and replanted.

With containers of beautiful roses, patios, decks and entryways can become colorful spaces.

Baby Blanket

Green Ice

Caring for Roses

WATERING

Watering is probably the most important maintenance practice for roses. Roses, especially repeat-blooming roses, need moisture for good blooming. If your soil has good drainage it is difficult to overwater. However, overwatering and overfeeding creates large flowers and lush growth, which are susceptible to attacks by insects and disease. The soil, wind, amount of sunlight, daylight temperature and amount of rainfall all must be considered when determining how much water to apply and when to apply it. Sandy soil will require more frequent watering than clay soil. It takes less time for water to reach the correct depth in sandy soil than in clay soil. Roses in windy locations will need more water than roses in sheltered locations. If the sun is particularly hot, the rose will need extra water.

Rainfall may not satisfy all the rose's water needs, especially in the hot valleys. A rain gauge indicates how much rain has fallen and will help you determine how much water you need to apply. Check your roses daily throughout the growing season. If the soil is dry several inches below the soil surface, it needs water. If you notice the leaves wilting, water immediately.

Container roses should be watered daily—water until the water comes out the holes in the bottom of the

Berkeley rose garden

container—though larger containers generally need water less often than smaller containers. Do not use a saucer or tray underneath any outdoor container. The saucer will trap water, which can drown the roots.

A general guideline is to apply 1" of water per week or about 5 gallons per plant. You will have to determine what watering regime is right for your area and soil composition. When you apply water, it should penetrate through the rootzone to a depth of at least 18". Shallow watering promotes root growth near the surface rather than deep root growth. Shallow roots may be damaged by cultivation or weeding, may suffer fertilizer burn and are susceptible to drought conditions.

Pristine

To determine if you are watering deeply enough, dig a hole beside the rose and see how far down the water has penetrated. Give the water at least half an hour to soak in before you check how far it has penetrated. If you watered for 15 minutes and the water has gone down 9", you know you need to water for a total of 30 minutes to get water to a depth of 18". Another method of measuring soil penetration is poking a stick into the watered soil. If the stick moves easily through the soil, the soil is wet enough; if the stick does not move easily, the soil is too dry. You can also use a soil probe, a hollow tube with a T-handle with the lower part of the hollow tube cut away on one side. Soil probes are available at irrigation supply businesses and some garden centers.

Europeana

Begin watering when natural rainfall has stopped and/or new growth begins to appear in canes. Your rose will not need as much water at the beginning of spring as it does in mid-summer, but you still must water deeply. In spring, water any dry beds and any roses under house eaves. Ease back on watering in fall to help the rose prepare itself for winter.

There are different ways to water. Using a hose and watering wand with a flood nozzle allows you to observe each rose close up. It is a great method but time consuming. Using sprinklers takes less of your time, but wind and evaporation affect the amount of water that reaches the rootzone. If you are using a sprinkler, it is best to water in the morning to give the foliage a chance to dry in the morning sun. Wet foliage is an invitation to fungal diseases. Watering in the morning also reduces the amount of evaporation that can occur when watering in the hot, afternoon sun. Soaker hoses are widely available at garden centers and hardware stores. They are easy to use and apply water directly to the rootzone without wetting the foliage.

Efficient watering techniques are especially important in areas with imposed water restrictions during hot and dry summers. You can reduce the amount of watering required by adding mulch and by using drought-tolerant roses such as rugosa, China or species roses.

MULCHING

Mulching refers to placing a layer of organic or inorganic material on top of the soil. Mulching slows evaporation, keeps roots cool, protects roots from damage from cultivation, suppresses weed growth and prevents soil-borne diseases from splashing onto the foliage. Mulching allows feeder roots to grow near the surface, increasing the rose's ability to absorb nutrients and water. Mulching prevents soil from crusting over or becoming compacted. Organic mulch also improves the soil as it decomposes, releasing nutrients and maintaining an open structure that encourages effective root penetration. Mulching also gives the bed a finished, natural appearance.

Organic mulches include compost, well-rotted manure (fresh manure can burn roots), pine and spruce needles, wood chips, shredded leaves, shredded bark, grass clippings and locally available agricultural byproducts, such as bedding from horse stables. Inorganic mulches include gravel, rocks, plastic and landscape fabric. Inorganic mulches can make winterizing and the subsequent spring cleanup very difficult. We recommend organic mulches for the benefit they provide to the soil.

Avoid using grass clippings as mulch. Bermuda grass is incredibly invasive and extremely difficult to eradicate, and if mulch of Bermuda grass is applied with stolons attached, it can root and grow. Cow manure can also contain Bermuda grass seeds that can germinate and cause the same problem. Avoid using peat moss alone as a mulch. It is very light and can blow away in the wind. Alone it dries quickly, and when dry it repels moisture. Mixed with other materials, peat moss is a suitable organic mulch.

Mulch may rob some nitrogen from the soil as it decomposes throughout the season. Compensate by applying a small amount of nitrogen fertilizer, such as fish fertilizer, when laying down the mulch. Avoid sawdust, especially from pressure-treated lumber and softwood trees, because it may release oils that retard plant growth. Avoid walnut leaves, large leaves and redwood mulch. Walnut leaves and redwood mulch are toxic to rose growth when they break down. Large leaves tend to mat together, restricting air and water movement. Shred and compost large leaves before using as mulch. Bark mulches should also be shredded because large chunks or nuggets leave spaces and allow weed seeds to fall in between and grow.

A good mulch allows air and water to penetrate the soil. Apply mulch to a depth of 3", thick enough to suppress weeds and still allow air circulation in the soil. Keep the mulch 1–2" away from the base of the rose.

FERTILIZING

Give your roses a good start by digging well-rotted manure or compost and any organic amendments prescribed by the soil test into the

Amber Queen in mulched bed

Melody Parfumeé

If you live in a big city, your roses may get covered in dust and pollutants, which inhibit photosynthesis. Wash roses once a week in the morning so the foliage dries quickly. Washing roses helps keep the spider mite and aphid populations down to a minimum.

soil during preparation (see Preparing the Soil, p. 34). Even if you have amended the soil for your roses before planting, you still need an ongoing program of fertilizing throughout the growing season.

Fertilizing roses is complex but not necessarily difficult. The fertility program for your roses depends on the type of roses you are growing and the nutrients available in your soil. Modern roses, such as hybrid teas and grandifloras, are heavy feeders that grow best in a rich, fertile soil. If you are growing species roses to naturalize an area, you will not fertilize to the same extent. If in doubt about fertilizing, a rose society in your area can provide information or put you in touch with someone who can help you develop a fertilizing program. A soil test will dictate the soil's needs. Don't just add fertilizer for the sake of adding it. You may end up feeding your roses to death; too much fertilizer will damage your rose.

The key to a successful fertility program is to feed the soil, not the plant. Healthy soils are dynamic ecosystems containing thousands of soil organisms that work in harmony with each other and the plants growing in them. Practices that disrupt the balance of the soil ecosystem can mean problems for plants. Perhaps the chemical fertilizer you used has changed the pH of the soil, making it difficult for soil microorganisms to thrive. They can no longer break down organic matter in the soil to provide the plant with nutrients, leaving your plant dependent on chemicals for nutrients. When the soil is out of ecological balance, harmful insects and diseases can move in. If you take care of your soil, it will produce good quality roses.

When to fertilize

Apply the first fertilization of the year when the leaves are at least one inch or more in size. Otherwise, you run the risk of burning the foliage. You can then proceed with a regular feeding program based on the product you've chosen and following the package directions. Apply the last fertilization of the year four to six weeks before the first frost. Frost can damage late, lush growth, so you don't want to fertilize too close to first frost. A safe approach is to stop using nitrogen fertilizers in mid-

Blaze Improved

summer and fertilize after that time with fall fertilizer, which is high in potassium.

Species roses, shrub roses and other once-flowering roses can be fertilized once a year in spring. The minimum fertilization for repeat bloomers is once in spring and once when the first flush of blooms is complete. Newly planted roses should be fertilized lightly six weeks after planting.

What to use

The numbers you see on a package or container of fertilizer, for example 24–14–14 or 20–24–14, represent nitrogen, phosphorous and potassium, respectively. The numbers are referred to as the 'fertilizer analysis.' The higher the number, the greater the amount of nutrient. A fertilizer with all three nutrients is called a complete fertilizer. A fertilizer specifically designed for roses contains the nutrients roses need the most. Follow the directions on the package for proper application rates, methods and precautions.

Climbing Cécile Brünner

Organic and chemical fertilizers are available in granular and liquid forms. Granular fertilizers are small, dry particles that can be easily spread by machine or hand. Granular chemical fertilizers have nitrogen available in either quick-release or slow-release formulations. Quick-release fertilizers provide a big shot of plant-available nitrogen in a short time. Too much nitrogen too quickly will favor foliage growth over flowers. It might burn the roots and the foliage. It might also create lush growth that is more vulnerable to insects and diseases if fungus is present. Slow-release fertilizers are a better choice because they release their nutrients over a long period, lowering the potential for burning, excessive vegetative growth and leaching of fertilizer into the groundwater. Granular organic fertilizers are naturally slow releasing. Many rosarians will supplement their slow-release fertility program with a small amount of quick-release nitrogen to ensure the rose is adequately fed.

Once-flowering: Fantin-Latour

Repeat-bloomer: Love

Liquid fertilizers come as liquid concentrate or powder that is mixed with water and applied to the soil or sprayed on the leaves. The most common soil-applied liquid fertilizer formulation is 20–20–20, but there are organic options available.

Organic fertilizers include compost, well-rotted manure, fish emulsion, fish meal, bloodmeal (high in nitrogen), alfalfa pellets, bonemeal, wood ashes and seaweed extracts. Organic fertilizers are better for the health of the soil and its inhabitants. For example, seaweed extracts such as kelp not only supply micronutrients, they also contain a substance that releases micronutrients already in the soil. When applied as a fertilizer in spring and fall, the seaweed extracts also help improve roses' cold hardiness and drought resistance. Fish emulsion and fish meal stimulate budding, blooming and foliage green-up. Fish emulsion can be used as a liquid feed throughout the growing season, applied right over the mulch. Fish meal can be gently scratched into the soil. Epsom salts (magnesium sulfate) are a good source of magnesium and sulfur, which is essential for chlorophyll production. Epsom salts encourage basal breaks, improve the production of blooms and boost the overall health of the plant. A good, balanced organic fertilizer mix for roses is three parts alfalfa meal, one part bonemeal and one part wood ash. Compost tea (see recipe) can be used as a liquid feed.

Spraying the leaves with fertilizer is called foliar feeding. It won't provide all the nutrition a rose needs but is good for supplementing a soil fertility program. Foliar feeding provides micronutrients, which are the nutrients required in smaller amounts. If your soil test reveals a need for micronutrients, a good form to use is chelated micronutrients sprayed on the foliage and onto the soil. Do not apply foliar feeds if temperatures are 90° F or higher.

Compost Tea Recipe
Mix a shovelful of compost in a 5-gallon bucket of water or a bucketful of compost in a 45-gallon barrel of water and let sit for a week. Dilute this mix, preferably with rainwater or filtered water, until it resembles weak tea. Best if used when watering or as a spray.

How to fertilize

If you are unsure about how much fertilizer to use, it is better to apply a little less fertilizer and a little more water. Most importantly, never fertilize a dry plant! Water the plant very well the day before you plan to fertilize to reduce the potential of burning.

Follow the directions that came with the fertilizer. Always wear gloves when using granular fertilizers. Measure the recommended amount of granular fertilizer, spread it out in a ring around the base of the rose (known as the "drip line") and lightly scratch the fertilizer into the soil with a cultivator or rake. Leave a 6–8" diameter of unfertilized area directly around the base of the rose so the fertilizer can reach the feeder roots.

Liquid fertilizers are mixed with water and poured onto the rootzone or sprayed onto the foliage. Hose-end sprayers, available at garden centers, department stores and some nurseries, make applying liquid fertilizers easy. Many rosarians use both granular and liquid fertilizers in various combinations.

Pierrine

PRUNING

Pruning is very important for roses. It is far healthier to prune a rose at least once a year than to not prune it at all. To prune effectively, you need to know why you are pruning, when to prune, how and where to make proper cuts, how to prune the specific rose you are growing and how to clean up after you are done.

Pruning removes any dead, diseased, damaged, interfering, crossing or rubbing canes. Pruning shapes the rose and keeps the center open to allow good air circulation. Pruning also keeps large roses from growing out of bounds. The natural growth habit for roses is to send basal breaks up from the base of the plant. These canes are vigorous and productive for a few years and then lose their vigor. The rose then channels its energy into producing new vigorous shoots. The older shoots still produce flowers, but they are small and of poor quality. Removing the older shoots allows the rose to channel all its energy into the new shoots and large, robust flowers.

When to prune

The best time to prune is January to mid-February, when the bud eyes begin to appear. At higher elevations, this cut-off date is later. It is never too late to prune, but pruning too early can be a mistake. Remove the old leaves and wait two weeks to begin pruning. After pruning, remove the leaves left on the canes.

Prune once-blooming roses, like species roses, after flowering is over. Because these roses bloom mostly or entirely on two-year-old wood, pruning them in winter removes the wood that produces flowers. Prune old garden roses when in bloom or immediately afterward. Once-flowering climbers can have flowering canes removed completely after flowering or the following winter.

Equipment for rose pruning

You will need the following tools to do a good pruning job:

Secateurs, or hand pruners, are used for cutting canes up to $3/4$" diameter. Using secateurs for cutting canes larger than $3/4$" in diameter increases the risk of damaging the remaining branch or stem and is physically more difficult for the person doing the pruning.

Loppers are long-handled pruners used for large, old canes up to $1^1/2$" in diameter.

Pruning saws can also be used for removing large, old canes. The teeth are designed to cut through green wood. Select a saw with a short blade, around 8", with a pointed tip. Choose a tapered blade for cutting in tight areas.

Puncture-proof leather gloves, preferably with leather extending up the forearm.

The cleaner and sharper the cut, the easier it is for the rose to heal the cut, so make sure your tools are sharp and clean before you begin pruning. If the cane you are cutting is diseased, you must sterilize the tool before using it again. A solution of 1 part bleach and 9 parts water is

Gift of Life in cutting bed

effective for cleaning and sterilizing. Hydrogen peroxide or isopropyl alcohol can be used instead of bleach. Some rosarians keep an aerosol can of cleaning solution in their tool kits for this purpose.

Bypass (scissors-type) secateurs and loppers provide a cleaner cut than non-bypass models. Anvil-type pruners have a cutting action similar to a cleaver and cutting board. The cuts from anvil pruners tend to be ragged, especially if the blade is dull.

Secateurs and loppers must be properly oriented when making a cut. The blade of the secateurs or loppers should be to the plant side of the cut and the hook should be to the side being removed. A cut made with

the hook on the plant side will be ragged and difficult to heal.

Identifying bud eyes

New shoots arise from the buds, or bud eyes, as well as from the base of the rose. Most pruning cuts will be made just above a bud. Buds are immediately above where a leaf was attached to the cane. At pruning time most buds are easily identified as little half-circle bulges on the cane. If the buds are a little hard to spot, especially on older canes, look for a horizontal, flat or crescent-shaped scar left by the leaf and assume a bud will develop just above it. New growth from buds occurs in the direction the bud is facing. When selecting a bud to cut back to, always select one that is on the side of the cane that faces away from the center of the plant. Your rose bush will have a nicer shape and you will keep the center of the rose bush open. Keeping the center of a rose clear allows air to flow through, which is a good defense against fungal diseases.

Latent buds, also known as dormant buds, are located on either side of a primary bud. They are stimulated when an actively growing cane is removed either deliberately or accidentally. They are easily removed by thumb pruning if you want to direct more of the plant's energy to the primary bud. You might want to

Hand pruners (secateurs) and loppers must be properly oriented when making a cut. The blade of the pruners or loppers should be to the plant side of the cut, and the hook should be to the side being removed. A cut made with the hook on the plant side will be ragged and difficult to heal.

leave them because latent buds may need to develop to replace old canes that are removed.

How to prune

In general, tender roses need less pruning and hardy roses need more. The following pruning is the minimum that all roses should have annually:

- Remove any dead, diseased, damaged or interfacing canes (canes crossing each other, rubbing together or growing into the center of the plant).
- If the rose is mature, remove two or more of the oldest, unproductive canes, but don't remove too many. Roses store a lot of energy in their canes in the form of unused nutrients and plant-produced sugars and proteins. The more canes that remain after pruning, the less the rose will have to rely on its roots to get going in spring.

If a rose has not been pruned for a few years and is gnarly and overgrown, don't cut it back all at once. Do the task over two years, by removing no more than one-third per year, to lessen the shock for the plant. After the first pruning, there will still be foliage producing energy and food for the plant. Successive hard pruning stresses the plant and limits the growth of the root system, which in turn limits the new growth above the ground.

Every four to five years, prune to renew the rose's branch structure. Work with the rose's natural growth habit. You will get a nicer looking, healthier rose when you follow the basic shape of the plant rather than work against it.

Pruning different varieties

Some of the more vigorous roses might benefit from additional pruning. A severe pruning every year is recommended for hybrid teas, grandifloras and floribundas. Ensure the center is opened and a nice vase-shaped plant outline is created. **Hybrid teas** should be pruned to three to five buds on three to five well-spaced canes. White and yellow hybrid teas are generally less vigorous plants, and should be pruned like floribundas and grandifloras. Prune **Floribundas** and **grandifloras** to five to seven buds on five to seven well-spaced canes.

Prune **miniatures** by at least one-half once they break dormancy, removing all weak and twiggy growth and any extra long canes or winter damage. Some rosarians cut them back to the lowest outward-facing bud on the previous year's growth.

Pruning for **shrub** roses involves mostly thinning and shaping. Prune in spring; do not prune after flowering other than to deadhead. Choose the rose to fit the space rather than having to constantly prune to keep the rose within bounds. Generally you can prune, to the crown or base, up to one-quarter of the old, unproductive canes annually on mature plants. Remove thin and twiggy

Pruning cuts for a hybrid tea

Pruning an old garden rose

Pruning a floribunda

growth (less than ¹/₄" in diameter) and all shoots lying on the ground. Shortening extra long canes on once-blooming varieties will stimulate flowering laterals.

Old garden roses should only be pruned once they've finished blooming. Repeat blooming old garden roses, notably bourbons, portlands and hybrid perpetuals, should be lightly shaped in winter at the same time as modern roses.

Climbing roses should not be pruned for two to three years after planting, other than to remove dead-wood, which allows the rose to produce long canes from which the flowering lateral branches will develop. Canes should be trained into position as they grow and mature. There are two aims when pruning climbers—encouraging growth of flowering lateral branches and initiating new main canes to replace old, unproductive canes. Annually remove one or two of the oldest canes (older than three years) and trim lateral branches to retain two to three bud eyes per lateral. Long canes can be trimmed to keep them within bounds.

If a main cane is growing in the wrong direction, make every attempt to train it into place. If it does not want to cooperate, remove the whole cane at the base. Long lateral branches may be treated as main canes.

After blooming, **rambling roses** produce many long, flexible canes from the base and long laterals from the canes that have just flowered. Next year's flowers arise from this new growth. Remove any canes that are not producing long, vigorous laterals after they have flowered. Remove once-flowering canes to the

Pruning cuts for a climber

New Dawn

base after flowering. Cut back laterals to 24–36" from the bud's main stem.

Repeat bloomers should be pruned after the last flush or in spring. Remove the flowering laterals to two to three buds from the main stem and remove one or two of the oldest canes to rejuvenate the rose. Train new canes to fill the space left from the removal of the old, unproductive canes. Any excess new growth can be removed from the base, but be careful to leave some growth to replace old canes.

Prune **groundcover roses** to keep them in the available space. If the groundcover rose is a creeping, stem-rooting variety, cut it well back from the boundary to an upward-facing bud or thin it out back to a main branch. Many groundcovers, such as Flower Carpet (p. 152), should be cut down to 10–12", which will rejuvenate the rose.

The goal for pruning **standard roses** is to have a nice balanced head. Shorten shoots by one-third. Ensure that the head is not too large or heavy to be supported. For weeping standards, remove stems that have finished flowering and leave the current season's growth undisturbed.

We recommend that rose-growers keep non-selective herbicides out of their gardens. It's better to pull weeds by hand than to suffer herbicide damage.

How to make proper pruning cuts

If pruning cuts are made correctly, the plant heals quickly, without disease and insect attacks. Pruning cuts for roses include (1) shortening canes to a bud or a branch and (2) removing old canes at the base.

When shortening a cane to a bud, the cut should be made to slightly less than 1/4" above a bud (see diagram). If the cut is too far away from or too close to the bud, the wound will not heal properly. Cut to a bud that is pointing away from the center of the rose. Shortening a cane to a branch is similar to shortening a cane to a bud. It is healthiest for the rose if the diameter of the cane you are cutting is at least one-third of the diameter of the branch you are cutting back to. The cut should be made at slightly less than 1/4" above the lateral branch and lined up with the angle of the branch (see diagram).

When removing an old cane at the base, always cut as close as you can to the base (or bud union if it is exposed). Any deadwood or stubs left on the rose are potential homes for insect pests and disease. In areas where there are rose cane borer attacks, the ends of the cut canes may be sealed with a little dab of white glue or pruning paste. Ensure the sealant is spread over the entire cut end. Sealants are unnecessary if borers are not a problem.

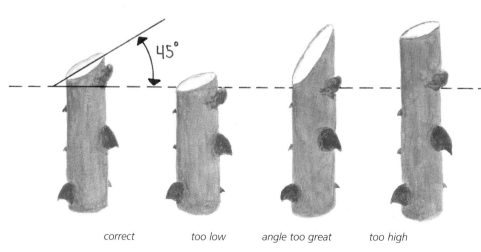

    correct   *too low*   *angle too great*   *too high*

Cutting back to a bud eye

Pegging down

Pegging down

Pegging down is the process of bending rose canes and pegging them to the ground near the tip of the cane. It is a way of controlling or training roses without actually cutting them. Roses are genetically programmed to grow to a certain height. Pegging the canes down tricks the rose into thinking it must send out new growth to attain that height. This is good for roses with long, flexible canes, especially hybrid perpetual and bourbon roses that tend to bloom only at the tips of their canes. Pegging down promotes flower production along the length of the cane.

In late summer or early fall, gently bend the canes over, cut the tips back to the first upward-facing bud from the tip and peg the canes to the ground with long, stiff wire staples. Use coat hangers bent in a U-shape or buy staples from a landscape supply business. Another method is to tie the canes to a low frame (no higher than 18"). The shoots created by pegging down should be pruned to 4–6" annually, in spring for repeat-blooming roses and after flowering for once-blooming roses.

Winter pruning in cold winter areas

The following section applies only to the small segment of Northern California rose-growers who live at higher elevations and experience cold winter conditions. These rose-growers should "top prune" their plants as winter approaches, thereby removing any long canes that may get damaged by strong winds.

In cold winter areas, the canes of only the hardiest roses survive above their protective cover or snowline. Remove winter-damaged wood by pruning back to healthy, outward-facing buds. Frost-damaged canes appear light brown to black with no green or reddish-brown color visible. Frost damage begins at the tip of the cane and works progressively down, sometimes right to the base. The pith of frost-damaged wood is brown. Healthy wood has white or slightly green pith. In older canes healthy pith may be a little off-white.

Begin cutting at the top of the cane and work down until you encounter healthy wood. The correct way to proceed is little by little, to prevent the removal of too much healthy wood. If you are not sure whether the cane is alive, leave it alone until new growth begins so you can see exactly what is happening with the canes. Old canes of rugosa roses may look frost damaged but are often still alive so should not be pruned away.

After-pruning care

After winter pruning, clean up around your roses. Remove any leaves remaining on the plant from the previous year. Clean up any debris and old leaves to remove insects and disease that may have overwintered in the debris.

During winter cleanup, many rosarians spray their roses and the soil with a lime-sulfur or lime-sulfur and oil mix to destroy any insect eggs or disease spores that might still be there. Roses must still be dormant when applying this spray. If your rose has already broken dormancy and started to shoot, spray only lime sulfur, as oil can damage the young shoots.

REMOVING SUCKERS

A sucker is a growth that arises from a plant's roots or underground stems. For grafted roses a sucker is unwanted growth that arises from the rootstock below the bud union. Watch for suckers throughout the growing season and remove them. They grow vigorously but do not flower and they sap energy from the variety above the graft union.

It's easy to spot suckers because the stem and foliage of the sucker will likely look different from the grafted variety. Remove a sucker and its latent buds by exposing the sucker

Unwanted rootstock suckers are growing to the left of this hybrid tea.

where it attaches to the root and pulling it sharply away from the root. It's best to pull the suckers completely off the rootstock.

It is easiest to remove suckers when they are still small. If the sucker is too large to pull off without damaging the root, then prune it off the root if possible. This is a temporary solution, however, as it will grow back. Cultivating carefully around the rootstock can also minimize suckers. Standard roses sucker along the stem. These suckers can be removed by hand as they sprout or sharply pulled off when they grow a little larger.

DEADHEADING

Deadheading is the process of removing spent blooms. It helps to keep plants looking clean and tidy and, for repeat bloomers, it encourages more blooms. When a rose plant finishes flowering it naturally wants

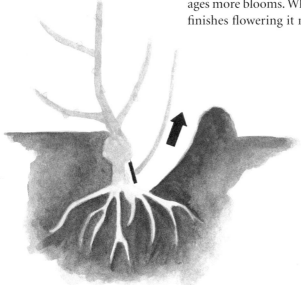

Cut a sucker off the rootstock of a grafted rose.

to produce seed-bearing hips, and when the rose is producing seed, it won't produce any more flowers. Removing the old blooms encourages the formation of new flowers, as the energy that would have gone into seed production is redirected to new bloom production.

Remove spent blooms as quickly as possible after they droop and fade. For large-flowered roses such as hybrid teas, cut the stem just above the first strong outward true leaf (five or more leaflets). The shoot that will emerge from the bud will grow outward, allowing for an open form that will improve air circulation and light penetration. The thicker the cane is where you make your deadheading cut, the stronger the new cane will be.

On weak canes or new plants, snap off the bloom to retain the maximum amount of foliage, which allows the canes to grow thicker and the plant to stay healthy.

For cluster-flowered roses such as floribundas, remove the entire cluster to just above the first strong outward true leaf (five or more leaflets).

Stop deadheading in late summer or early fall, four to six weeks before the first frost date, to allow for hip production, which signals the plant to prepare for dormancy.

It is better to not deadhead once-blooming roses. Removing the flowers inhibits production of hips. Many once-blooming roses have attractive hips that provide good fall and winter color as well as food for birds and other wildlife.

Deadheading

Propagation

If you have developed a passion for growing roses, you may want to move to the next level and begin propagating your own roses. There are many reasons to propagate your own roses, including developing new varieties and sharing roses with other gardeners. Following are brief discussions of some of the techniques used to propagate more plants. More information can be found in other print sources. See the Resources on page 262.

Roses are propagated by budding, cuttings, seed or, for some roses, ground layering. Budding is the most common means of commercially propagating roses. Budding is the process of inserting a leaf bud of one rosebush under the bark of a rootstock variety. It has to be done in a very particular manner and requires practice.

When creating a new variety, rose breeders pollinate one rose variety with pollen from another and grow hybrid plants from the resulting seeds. This is known as hybridizing.

The process of seeding roses is similar to seeding any perennial or woody ornamental, with the seeds of roses taken from the ripe hips. Seeding most often produces variable seedlings, with different colors, forms and so on, depending on what parentage was used.

Roses grown from cuttings are genetically identical to the plant the cuttings were taken from, so propagation by cuttings is used when you want more of a certain variety of rose. Patented roses are protected by plant

patent laws for 20 years and must not be reproduced by any means.

Ground layering allows future cuttings to form their own roots before they are removed from the parent plant. A section of a flexible branch is buried until it produces roots, at which time it is removed from the parent plant. This method works well with lax-stemmed roses such as albas, damasks, bourbons and some species roses.

If you have own-root roses, you can take advantage of the naturally occurring suckers. Let the sucker grow until it develops roots of its own. The sucker can then be removed and planted to a new location. It's kind of like automatic ground layering without all the work.

ground layering

Gold Medal is a patented grandiflora rose.

Problems & Pests

There is both good and bad when it comes to roses and pests and diseases. Many insects and diseases attack only one plant species while others, such as aphids, have a variety of hosts. Mixed plantings can make it more difficult for pests to find their preferred hosts and establish a population. At the same time, because roses are in the same spot for many years, problems can become permanent. The advantage is that beneficial insects, birds and other pest-devouring organisms can also develop permanent populations.

For many years pest control meant spraying or dusting, with the goal of eliminating every pest in the landscape. A more moderate approach that many gardeners advocate today is known as IPM (Integrated Pest Management or Integrated Plant Management). The goal of IPM is to reduce pest problems to levels at which only negligible damage is done by incorporating cultural, physical, biological and, as a last resort, chemical means of control. Of course, gardeners must determine what degree of damage is acceptable to them. Someone growing hybrid tea roses for exhibition will tolerate far less damage than someone growing species roses in a woodland garden. Consider whether a pest's damage is localized or covers the entire plant. Will the damage kill the plant or is it affecting only the outward appearance? Are there methods of controlling the pests without chemicals?

A good IPM program includes learning about your plants, the conditions they need for healthy growth, what pests might affect them, where and when to look for those pests and how to control them. Keep records of pest damage because your observations can reveal patterns useful in spotting recurring problems and in planning your maintenance regime.

Proper identification of what is affecting your rose will help you take appropriate corrective measures.

Healthy roses can resist most pests & diseases.

Insects, disease or nutrient deficiencies can cause problems. If you are unsure what is happening to your rose, contact your local rose society, local garden center or the University of California's cooperative extension service. Other post-secondary schools and the Internet are also good sources for information.

Choose roses of top quality that are resistant to the major diseases in your area. Many beautiful disease-resistant varieties are available. Hybridizers are working at breeding back in the resistance that was being somewhat lost in the quest for the perfect flower form. If you want to grow rose varieties that are susceptible to disease, you may need to tolerate a less-than-perfect rose or find a way to minimize the damage. A good way to determine which roses best suit your garden is to contact a local rose society. Consulting rosarians are usually available to help with your selection needs. You could also visit a rose garden or walk through your neighborhood and observe which roses are growing well.

There are four steps in effective and responsible pest management. Cultural controls are the most important. Physical controls should be attempted next, followed by biological controls. Resort to chemical controls only when the first three possibilities have been exhausted. They can endanger the gardener and his or her family and pets and kill as many good organisms as bad, leaving the garden more vulnerable.

Leaves afflicted with blackspot

A healthy rose is simply the best defense against pest or disease.

Cultural controls are the gardening techniques you use in the daily care of your garden. Make sure your roses have adequate light, water and air circulation. Ensure the soil has adequate drainage, plenty of organic matter and nutrients and an ideal soil pH. Prevent the spread of disease and insects by keeping gardening tools clean. Thoroughly clean and remove fallen leaves and dead plant matter throughout the season, especially in fall. Providing the conditions roses need for healthy growth reduces plant stress. A stressed plant is vulnerable to pests and disease.

Physical controls are generally used to combat insect problems. An example of such a control is picking insects off plants by hand, which is not as daunting as it sounds if you catch the problem when it is just beginning. Simply squishing the insects is another method. Other physical controls include barriers that stop insects from reaching the plant and traps that catch or confuse insects. Physical control of diseases often necessitates removing the infected plant part or parts to prevent the spread of the problem. Burn the infected material or take it to a permitted disposal site.

Biological controls make use of populations of predators that prey on pests. Birds, snakes, frogs, spiders, ladybird beetles (ladybugs) and certain bacteria can play an important role in keeping pest populations at a manageable level. Encourage these creatures to take up permanent residence in your garden. A birdbath and birdfeeder will encourage birds to enjoy your yard and feed on a variety of insect pests. Beneficial insects are probably already living in your landscape, and you can encourage them to stay by planting appropriate food sources. Many beneficial insects eat nectar from flowers such as perennial yarrow. Biological insects

Frogs eat many insect pests.

are available for purchase from various organic control suppliers as well.

Another form of biological control is the naturally occurring soil bacterium *Bacillus thuringiensis* var. *kurstaki*, or *B.t.* for short (commercially available), which breaks down the gut lining of some insect pests. It is available in garden centers.

Chemical controls should be used only as the last alternative to pest and disease management, but if you must use them, choose from the available organic options. Organic sprays are no less dangerous than chemical ones, but they will break down into harmless compounds. The main drawback to chemicals is that they may also kill the beneficial insects you have been trying to attract to your garden. Organic chemicals are available at most garden centers. Follow the manufacturer's instructions carefully and apply no more than the recommended amount. Note that if a particular pest or disease is not listed on the package, it will not be controlled by that product. Proper and early identification is vital to finding a quick solution. Alternate different spray products so the pest won't build up a resistance to the chemical. Follow these guidelines with any chemical usage, including pesticides, insecticides and fungicides.

You can apply fungicides as a preventive measure when conditions are right for disease growth or after you see the disease on your rose. You can choose between organic and chemical fungicides. Both are effective, but organic fungicides are far better for the environment. If you feel a need to use chemical fungicides, check with the local garden center or rose society for the appropriate information. At all times follow the directions on the product label. And remember: more is not better.

Many consumers are demanding effective pest products that do not harm the environment. Biopesticides are made from plants, animals, bacteria and minerals. Microbial pesticides contain bacteria, fungi, viruses and other microbes as their active ingredients. Plant pesticides are derived from naturally occurring plant compounds. Biochemical pesticides come from other naturally occurring substances that control pests by non-toxic means. They are much less harmful than conventional pesticides and for the most part target only the pest. They are effective in small quantities and decompose quickly in the environment. Hopefully these products will reduce our reliance on chemical pesticides.

The recipes on the next pages incorporate commonly available ingredients. Many gardeners use these types of homemade mixtures as alternatives to commercially available pesticides. When used responsibly they have no adverse effects on the environment. Please note that these homemade mixtures are not to be packaged, distributed or sold.

Apple cider vinegar

The following mixture can be used to treat leaf spot, mildew and blackspot.

In a spray bottle, mix:

3 tablespoons cider vinegar (5 percent acidity)

1 gallon water

Spray on the foliage, including undersides, every 2–3 days for a total of 3 applications.

Baking soda & horticultural oil

University studies have confirmed the effectiveness of this mixture against powdery mildew.

In a spray bottle, mix:

4 teaspoons baking soda

1 tablespoon horticultural oil

1 gallon water

Spray on the foliage, including undersides, every 3–4 days for a total of 3 applications. Do not pour or spray this mix directly into the soil.

Baking soda & citrus oil

The following mixture treats both blackspot and powdery mildew.

In a spray bottle, mix:

4 teaspoons baking soda

1 tablespoon citrus oil

1 gallon water

Spray on the foliage, including undersides, every 2–3 days for a total of 3 applications. Do not pour or spray this mix directly into the soil.

Garlic spray

This spray is an effective, organic means of controlling aphids, leafhoppers, whiteflies and some fungi and nematodes.

Soak:

6 tablespoons finely minced garlic in 2 teaspoons mineral oil for a minimum of 24 hours

Add:

1 pint of water and $1^1/_2$ teaspoons of liquid dish soap

Stir and strain into a glass container for storage. Combine 1–2 tablespoons of this concentrate with 2 cups water to make a spray. Test the spray on a couple of leaves and check after two days for any damage from the soap/garlic mixture. If there is no damage, then you can spray your rose thoroughly, ensuring good coverage of the foliage. One to two applications should be sufficient.

Milk spray

Milk spray helps prevent and control blackspot and mildew. It has been tested on roses and a variety of vegetables and has been moderately successful. Any kind of milk can be used, from high fat milk to skim and even powdered milk. Milk with a lower fat content is recommended as it will have less of an odor. Mix one part milk with nine parts water and apply in a spray every five to seven days for a total of three applications.

Fish emulsion/seaweed (kelp)

These products are usually used as foliar nutrient feeds but appear to also work against fungal diseases by either preventing the fungus from spreading to non-infected areas or by changing the growing conditions for the fungus.

Neem oil

Neem oil is derived from the neem tree (from India) and is used as an insecticide, miticide and fungicide. It works best as a preventive measure. Apply when conditions are favorable for disease development. Neem is virtually harmless to most beneficial insects and microorganisms.

Antitranspirants

These products were developed to reduce water transpiration, or loss of water, in plants. The waxy polymers also surround fungal spores, preventing the spread of spores to nearby leaves and stems. When applied according to label directions, antitranspirants are environmentally friendly.

Sulfur and lime-sulfur

These products work well as preventive measures. You can get ready-made products or wettable powders that you mix yourself. Do not spray when the temperature reaches 90° F or higher as doing so can damage the plant.

Bordo Fungicides

These products can be used to treat fungal problems including blackspot, powdery mildew and rust. They are available in wettable powders and are easily applied either dry or wet. Follow the recommended rates and instructions to prevent the foliage from being burned.

Be careful if you are using copper mixtures, including Bordo fungicides. They may effectively control fungal disease for the entire season but can be damaging to the soil and toxic to the user.

The foliage of this White Meidiland has blackspot.

Spray only well-watered plants before 10 A.M. or after 4 P.M.

GLOSSARY OF PESTS & DISEASES

The following glossary includes brief descriptions of some of the pests and diseases that may occur from time to time. It can be helpful to further explore identification of pests and their lifecycles, their most damaging stages and the best methods of reducing the damage. Check the list of resources on page 262 or contact your local library, rose or garden club, the Internet or garden center for additional information.

Aphids

Tiny, pear-shaped insects, winged or wingless; black, brown, green, red or gray. Cluster along stems, buds and leaves but are most often found on new, tender growth. Suck sap from plants; cause distorted or stunted growth. Aphids produce honeydew, a sticky, sugary fluid deposited on leaves and stems. Sticky honeydew forms on surfaces and encourages black, sooty mold growth. Aphids are like 'plant lice' and are the most common rose insect pests and likely the easiest to control. Aphids are not present during hot summers, but they often return as days get cooler and shorter.

What to Do. Squish small colonies by hand; dislodge them with brisk water spray; spray serious infestations with insecticidal soap; many predatory insects and birds feed on them. An application of dormant oil will kill overwintering eggs.

Armillaria Root Rot (Shoestring Fungus, Oak Root Fungus)

Soil-borne, parasitic fungus; causes decay of roots and crown by breaking down tissue. May kill the plant quickly or slowly. Plants exhibit stunted growth. Leaves turn yellow or brown; plant wilts then dies, often one stem or branch at a time. White fungal strands appear under the bark near the crown and on the roots. Honey-colored mushrooms appear around the base of the plant during wet weather. Attacks are most frequent in heavy, clay soils with poor drainage. It is most harmful and prevalent in oaks. Weakened or stressed plants are also vulnerable.

What to Do. Avoid planting susceptible plants where the fungus is

Aphids

known to exist. Ensure good surface and sub-surface drainage. When preparing a planting area, remove all old tree and shrub roots and mix in a large amount of rich compost. Remove and destroy infected plants and re-plant only resistant plants.

Bacterial Canker

Enters the rose through wounded stem tissue and can attack any part of the rose. Weakened roses more susceptible. Red or yellow spots on the stem progress to form brown patches and lesions that shrivel and die. If the disease is severe enough it will girdle the stem, killing all growth above the infected area.

What to Do. Maintain plant vigor. Avoid wounds on plants. Control borers. Prune out and destroy diseased branches (see pruning p. 58). Sterilize your pruning equipment after each cut. Remove rubbing or crossing branches annually.

Beetles

Many types and sizes; usually round with hard, shell-like outer wings that cover membranous inner wings. Some types are beneficial, e.g., ladybird beetles ('ladybugs'); others are not. Both the adult insects and the larvae feed on roses and other garden plants. Rose Curculio, sometimes known as Rose Weevil, drills holes in the buds. Cucumber Beetle feeds on the petals. Larvae feed on roots and other organic materials in the soil. Hoplia beetles can become pests in early spring. All

Ladybird beetles are beneficial insects in the garden.

of these overwinter in the soil, so the soil itself may need treatment.

What to Do. Remove by hand and drop in a container of soapy water. Spread an old sheet under the rose plant and shake off beetles to collect and dispose of them. Spray insecticidal soap or pyrethrin (plant-based insecticides) on visible insects. Plant repellent herbs and perennials as companions: catmint, chamomile, garlic, lavender, rosemary, garden sage, painted daisy, tansy and thyme. Plant radishes to attract beetles away from the roses. Treat soil with parasitic nematodes, spray roses with beneficial insect sprays, repellents like garlic water, neem oil and other registered pesticides or beneficial bacteria. Kill larvae with diatomaceous earth. Dust with Rotenone. Prune out infected portions and destroy.

Blackspot

The most prevalent fungal disease in roses. The fungus overwinters in infected leaves and canes, so plant sanitation is important. Most problematic when warm, humid weather (70°–80° F) is sustained for over a week. Can cause weak growth and stems to die back. An infestation by a single spore can produce visible colonies in as little as 15 days. First appears on the lower foliage as black or brown blotches; yellow rings form to outline the blotches. Badly infected foliage drops; severe cases can defoliate a rose.

What to Do. Keep the area free of fallen infected leaves. Remove all the leaves before winterizing to prevent overwintering spores. Use a preventive fungicide when the environmental conditions are favorable for fungal infection. The spores are too small to see before they infect the leaf. Take extra care to spray the undersides of the leaves. Funginex and Daconil are common and effective chemical controls; use them only when all else fails.

Botrytis

Fungal disease that occurs in high humidity. Affects the stems and flowers of mature roses and the bare roots of poorly stored or shipped plants. Grayish-brown fuzzy mold on stems and flower buds; grayish-brown lesion runs down one side of the bud and onto the stem; red spots on petals. Flower buds may not open or if they open partially, the petal edges may appear soft and brown.

What to Do. Plant the rose where the morning sun can dry the plant; remove and destroy any infected plant parts. Improve the air circulation around and through the plant. Do not mulch over the crown. Daconil has proven effective as well.

Rose heavily afflicted with blackspot

Cane Borers

The term "cane borer" is an umbrella term that encompasses many different types of insects that burrow through canes. These are usually insect larva, and they cause the cane to wilt and die. Look for a small hole in the tip of the cane as evidence of a cane borer. Common borers include the stem-boring sawfly and several cane-nesting wasps and bees.

What to do. Cut out and destroy infected canes. Often the cane was weak or dead to begin with, long before the borer invaded it.

Caterpillars

Larvae of butterflies, moths. Include budworms, cutworms, leaf rollers, corn earworms, rose slugs and webworms. Chew foliage and buds. Severe infestions can completely defoliate a plant.

What to Do. Use high-pressure water and soap or pick caterpillars off by hand. Cut off large tents or webs of larvae. Control biologically using the naturally occurring soil bacterium *Bacillus thuringiensis* var. *kurstaki*, or *B.t.* for short (commercially available), which breaks down gut lining of caterpillars. Apply dormant oil in spring. Plants such as cornflower, purple coneflower or passion vine will attract the caterpillars away from roses; use neem oil or organic and synthetic pesticides; release parasitic wasps; encourage predatory insects with nectar plants such as yarrow. Diatomaceous earth is an effective control. Chemical controls include Rotenone. As a last resort, remove the infected plant.

Disinfecting tools

Dip pruning tools into denatured alcohol or a solution of 1 part liquid chlorine bleach and 9 parts water. Disinfect tools between each plant when pruning non-infected plants; between each cut when pruning infected plants. After disinfecting tools, scrub any discolored areas with steel wool, sharpen the cutting edges and oil metal surfaces. A pressurized can of cleaning solution also works well to disinfect.

Crown Gall

Unusual wart-like swellings of plant tissues caused by bacteria; more prevalent on grafted roses; growth begins at the base of the plant or on the bud union. Bacteria in the soil enter through wounds in the root and crown. Makes tissue green and pliable before forming into dark, crusty growths on roots or crown. Stunts growth, restricts water and nutrient uptake and reduces foliage and bloom production. Easily spread by infected tools.

What to Do. Remove any plants that have galls. Replace contaminated soil. Some report success with pruning away galls and spraying the infected area with anti-bacterial solutions or copper compounds. Pouring a few small drops of bleach over the wound, or applying it with a cotton swab, can also work.

Insecticidal soap recipe

*You can make your own
insecticidal soap.*

*Mix 1 teaspoon mild dish soap,
with little to no fragrance or
color, or pure soap
(biodegradable options are
available) with 1 quart water in a
clean spray bottle.*

*Spray the surface areas of your
plants.*

*Rinse them well within one hour
of spraying.*

Leaf Cutter Bee

Cuts neat, smooth circles from the edges of leaves.

What to Do. Nothing. As a pollinator, it is a beneficial insect. Damage is only aesthetic.

Leafhoppers

Small, wedge-shaped insects, often green, but can be brown, gray or multi-colored. Jump around frantically when disturbed. Suck juice from plant leaves and cause distorted growth. Like aphids, they can transmit diseases from plant to plant as they feed. Immature leafhoppers feed on undersides of leaves.

What to Do. Encourage predators by planting nectar-producing plants. Wash insects off with strong spray of water; spray with insecticidal soap.

Rosa eglanteria

Mildew

Two types, both caused by fungus, but with slightly different symptoms. *Downy mildew:* may be confused with blackspot. One of the most feared rose diseases, although rare; has shown isolated infection in some areas in Northern California. Prefers cool, moist or humid conditions with splashing water and wind to carry its spores to the next host. Two days of dry, hot weather (90° F or higher) will stop the disease, but spores remain for future infections. Purple-red irregular blotches on the new leaf and stem growth are systemic; lesions are a sign that the disease has spread throughout the plant. Gray fuzz on undersides of the foliage. *Powdery mildew:* attacks many rose varieties in all climates but prefers warm, moist, cloudy days and cool, humid nights. Less destructive than downy mildew. Appears on young leaves, stems and thorns. Begins as pinkish lesions and changes into a white or gray powdery coating. Canes can become distorted and flower petals appear dry and become discolored on the edges. Severe infestations may lead to new growth being distorted and dying.

What to Do. Choose roses that are not susceptible to mildew. Fall cleanup is essential to prevent mildew from overwintering on canes and fallen leaves. Provide good air circulation. Remove and destroy any infected foliage. Apply fungicides such as lime-sulfur or dormant oil while the rose is dormant in winter.

Bordo is another effective fungicide. Spray the soil as well to decrease overwintering active spores. There is no chemical control.

Nematodes

Tiny worms that cannot be seen with the naked eye; give plants disease symptoms. Plant growth is stunted and does not respond to water or fertilizer. Roots have tiny bumps, galls or knots.

What to Do. Mulch soil, add lots of organic matter, clean up debris in fall. Can add parasitic nematodes to soil or treat soil with neem. Remove infected plants in extreme cases. Plant nematode-resistant plants. Sterilize the soil with black plastic prior to planting (see p. 45).

Powdery mildew

Root Rot

Fungus that can cause weak, stunted growth. Leaves yellow and plant wilts and dies. Digging up plant will show rotted roots.

What to Do. Keep soil well drained. Do not overwater. Don't damage plant if you are digging around it; keep mulches away from base. Destroy plant if whole plant infected.

Rose Midge

Small, nearly invisible adult insects; hatch at the growing tips and use their rasping mouth parts to feed on tender new tissue, especially flower buds. Rose shrivels or bears no flowers, but the rest of the plant is healthy. Other evidence is scorched or blackened newer growth, blind tips and no buds. The symptoms are most evident in May through September, in Sonoma and Marin counties. Rose midge overwinters in soil.

Leaves with rose mosaic virus

What to Do. Difficult to control. Prune out and destroy blackened buds and canes; make sure to prune back hard to get rid of larvae that may have traveled down the cane. Add predatory nematodes to the soil to destroy the pupating larvae. Place a sheet of black plastic around the base of the rose to stop the larvae from reaching the soil to pupate. Keep the area around the plant free of weeds and litter. It may be helpful to also consult a local rosarian, garden center or nursery or the University of California's cooperative extension service for other solutions.

Rose Mosaic

Viral disease. Often confused with a nutrient deficiency, interveinal chlorosis. Yellow, irregular rings, line or netting patterns appear on leaf. Weakens plant, making it vulnerable to other pests and environmental stresses. Blooms may be distorted or undersized; early leaf drop may occur. Not transmitted by insects but can be transmitted by infected pruning tools and grafting.

What to Do. Remove the rose and replace the soil. Inform the people who sold you the plant that the plant had a virus. Contact suppliers to check if there has been any infected stock reported. Reputable suppliers will give you this information.

Rust

Bright orange spots on leaf undersides; brown spots on upper leaf surfaces. Severe infestations appear as

Rose hips and leaves covered in rust

lesions and attack stems. New growth becomes distorted. Can cause complete defoliation if left unchecked. More common in mild, wet weather (65°–70° F) including humid and foggy days and heavy morning dew. Spores are transmitted by wind and water and will overwinter. No roses are immune to rust.

What to Do. Pick off and destroy infected leaves. Where the disease is common, spray weekly with sulfur in early spring. Prune at least 1" beyond the non-infected tissue.

Spider Mites

Tiny, eight-legged relatives of spiders; do not eat insects but may spin webs. Almost invisible to the naked eye; red, yellow or green; usually found on underside of leaves. Suck juice out of leaves. May see fine webbing on leaves and stems; may see mites moving on leaf undersides. Leaves become discolored and speckled, then turn brown and shrivel up. Spider mites prefer hot, dry weather; roses next to walls and those under drought stress are vulnerable to attack.

Spider mites on red rose

Severe infestations can completely defoliate the plant.

What to Do. Wash off with strong water spray, especially targeting the undersides of leaves, until all signs of infestation are gone. Spray plants with insecticidal soap; ensure roses receive a deep and thorough watering as water-stressed plants are inviting to these creatures. Special miticides (insecticide specific to mites) are available. Predatory mites can be ordered through commercial insectiaries. Check the Biological Producers Association website for recommendations.

Thrips

Tiny, flying insects. Scrape the flower surfaces and suck the juice from the open wounds. Damage is mainly on buds and open blooms. Petals appear bruised and discolored with light brown, translucent spots especially around the petal edges. Flowers can be deformed and buds can fail to open. Thrips prefer tight, full buds of large-flowered yellow, pink or white roses. They thrive in hot and dry weather.

What to Do. Remove and destroy infected plant parts; encourage native predatory insects; spray serious infestations with insecticidal soap. Spunbound polyester covers can be effective.

Whiteflies

Tiny, white insects that flutter up into the air when the plant is disturbed. May appear as white dust above the foliage; tend to live near the top of the plant. Pierce the tissue and suck plant juices, causing yellowed leaves and weakened plants; produce honeydew. Damage may also include loss of foliage and stunted growth.

What to Do. Destroy weeds where insects may live. Encourage predatory insects and parasitic wasps. Spray severe infestations with insecticidal soap. Can use sticky traps, pheromone traps or light traps. Organic pesticides such as neem oil, horticultural oil and garlic water may be used.

Beneficial predatory ground beetle

OTHER PROBLEMS
Blind Shoots

Sometimes shoots will arise that have no terminal flower buds. These are known as blind shoots. They take energy away from flower production.

What to Do. Cut back blind shoots to the first five-leaflet leaf with an outward-facing bud and hope it produces a flowering shoot. If you prefer, you can leave the blind shoots alone to retain more foliage.

Heat stress

Major cause of yellowing leaves. Most noticeable during sudden temperature changes, especially on young plants and new growth. Leaf margins may scorch. Blooms may have darkened petal edges.

What to Do. Spray plants with anti-transpirants/anti-desiccants; screen new plants from sun; plant roses out of afternoon sun; apply mulch to keep roots cool; run overhead sprinkler during the heat of the day.

Mechanical problems

Cultivating too close to the roots can damage them; damaged roots reduce water and nutrient uptake and encourage suckers. Be aware of yellowing foliage and of any roots visible after cultivating.

What to Do. Take care when cultivating, going no deeper than 1–2"; prune freshly exposed roots and re-plant; water deeply so roots penetrate below normal cultivation depths.

Salt stress

Accumulated salts compete with rose roots for moisture and can make required nutrients unavailable (nutrient fixation) to plants, even though the nutrient is available in the soil. The result is yellowed leaves, reduced plant growth, scorched leaf margins and eventually plant death. Container roses are most susceptible. The regular use of water-soluble fertilizers may lead to salt buildup, especially where soils are heavy or where irrigation or rainfall fails to wash these salts past the rootzone. Water high in phosphates may also cause salt buildup.

What to Do. Irrigate deeply; improve drainage; get soil tests done regularly; change soil in containers every three to four years.

Water stress

Excess water: veins in the leaves begin to turn yellow, then the entire leaf yellows and droops; blooms fail to open completely; pith becomes soft and brown. *Inadequate water:* leaf margins wilt and scorch.

What to Do. Improve drainage; increase or decrease water as needed.

Nutrient Deficiencies

Sometimes what may look like pest or disease damage may be a nutrient deficiency or toxicity. A soil test or a plant tissue test is the only way to tell for sure if there is a nutrient deficiency or toxicity.

Boron is responsible for water movement within the plant. A deficiency manifests itself as mottled, yellow, misshapen new leaves and buds that are growing too close to each other at the top of the plant.

Calcium is a nutrient in liming materials used to increase soil pH. Calcium deficiency occurs in younger or upper leaves. Leaves brown, curl, shrivel and die. Phosphorus and iron aren't available to the plant when there is an excess of calcium.

Iron deficiency, or iron chlorosis, produces interveinal yellowing of new growth and younger leaves at the top of the plant. Iron contributes to the production of chlorophyll.

Magnesium deficiency looks like iron deficiency, but the yellow leaves with dark veins occur on the older, lower leaves first. Magnesium is a common nutrient in some liming materials used to increase soil pH.

Manganese regulates metabolic processes. Manganese deficiency resembles magnesium deficiency, but the younger leaves appear webbed or net-like. The new leaves may be spotted and older leaves mottled. Excess manganese reduces iron uptake.

Nitrogen encourages vegetative growth and is responsible for a plant's overall size. It is the nutrient most commonly deficient because it leaches from the soil, especially in

Rainbow's End

sandy soils. Nitrogen deficiency appears as undersized, pale green to yellow leaves, and affects the older leaves first. Stems may be weak and thin and blooms may be small. Overall plant growth is slow and stunted. Excess nitrogen causes overly lush, dark green growth and weak stems that are susceptible to attack by insects, disease and winterkill.

Phosphorus encourages root development and is very rarely deficient. A phosphorus deficiency begins as dark green to purplish coloration in the older, lower leaves. Overall plant growth is stunted and spindly. Phosphorus toxicity causes yellowing of the leaves between the veins. The leaves may be thicker, stems may be shorter and buds may be malformed or curled. Phosphorus accumulates in the soil, especially in heavy soils.

Potassium promotes flowering, plant strength and structure and therefore improves resistance to potential problems. It contributes to chlorophyll production. Potassium deficiency is seen first on the older, lower leaves. The leaves begin to yellow between the veins from the leaf tips and margins (leaf edge) and the edges begin to brown. Potassium toxicity is similar to phosphorus toxicity except that too much potassium results in root loss and therefore affects the plant's ability to take up water and nutrients.

Sulfur is commonly added to the soil (a different formulation of sulfur is used as a fungicide) to lower pH over time. It encourages the production of chlorophyll (responsible for the green color in leaves). Sulfur deficiency occurs on new growth. The leaves and leaf veins turn yellow and the roses become stunted. Excessive sulfur causes the leaf veins to turn yellow, followed by rapid loss of the lower leaves.

Zinc promotes water uptake. A deficiency appears as an interveinal chlorosis (yellowing between the veins), stunted growth, smaller foliage, thick stems, rosetting of new shoots and a whitish appearance. An excess of zinc reduces the uptake of manganese.

Ladybird beetle (ladybug) larva

Bonica

Ballerina

Rosa glauca

Easy-to-grow Roses

Groundcover roses
Species roses
Ballerina
Bonica
Buff Beauty
Carefree Wonder
Cupcake
Electron
Flower Carpet
Gourmet Popcorn
Madame Hardy
New Dawn
St. Patrick
Queen Elizabeth
Sexy Rexy
Simplicity
Sombreuil
Stainless Steel
Tournament of Roses

Shade-tolerant Roses

American Pillar
Ballerina
Blanc Double de Coubert
Bonica
Buff Beauty
Charles de Mills
Felicia
Félicité Parmentier
French Lace
Frau Dagmar Hastrup
Golden Wings
Heritage
Mutabilis
New Dawn
Ralph's Creeper
Rosa glauca
The Fairy

Drought-tolerant Roses

Groundcover roses
Species roses
Europeana
Harison's Yellow
Mister Lincoln
Stanwell Perpetual

Disease-resistant Roses

Groundcover roses
Species roses
Altissiino
Blanc Double de Coubert
Bonica
Carefree Wonder
Cherry Parfait
Dainty Bess
Dortmund
Elina
Fantin Latour
Félicité Parmentier
Fourth of July
Frau Dagmar Hastrup
Gizmo
Iceberg
Lavender Lassie
Mellow Yellow
Pat Austin
Rosarium Uetersen
Rosy Outlook
The Fairy
The Mayflower
White Meidiland

Fourth of July

Elina

Heritage

Red (Dublin Bay)

Pink (Jacques Cartier)

Yellow (Graham Thomas)

Red

Linda Campbell
Prospero
Ralph's Creeper
Red Ribbons
Altissimo
Blaze Improved
Don Juan
Dortmund
Dublin Bay
Liebeszauber
Fragrant Cloud
Mister Lincoln
Veteran's Honor
Europeana
Hot Cocoa
Lavaglut
Trumpeter
Love
Gizmo
Glowing Amber
Miss Flippins
Starina

Pink

Rosa eglanteria
Rosa glauca
Rosa virginiana
Charles de Mills
Fantin-Latour
Félicité Parmentier
Jaques Cartier
Louise Odier
Reine des Violettes
Stanwell Perpetual
Ballerina
Bonica
Carefree Wonder
China Doll
Frau Dagmar Hastrup
Heritage

Lavender Lassie
Mary Rose
Outta the Blue
The Fairy
The Mayflower
Thérèse Bugnet
Baby Blanket
Ferdy
Flower Carpet
Nozomi
Albertine
America
American Pillar
Belle of Portugal
Climbing Cécile
   Brünner
Dainty Bess
Diana Princess of
   Wales
Electron
New Dawn
Rosarium Uetersen
Barbra Streisand
Bride's Dream
Elizabeth Taylor
Gemini
Gift of Life
Memorial Day
New Zealand
Lady of the Dawn
Sexy Rexy
Simplicity
Queen Elizabeth
Tournament of Roses
Cupcake
Giggles
Minnie Pearl
Pierrine
Winsome

Yellow

R. banksiae lutea
Harison's Yellow
Mutabilis (turns pink,
    then crimson)
Buff Beauty
Golden Celebration
Golden Wings
Graham Thomas
Pat Austin
Flutterbye
Golden Showers
Mellow Yellow
Peace
St. Patrick
Easy Going
Playboy
Sunsprite
Gold Medal
Fairhope
Rise 'n' Shine

White/Cream

Madame Hardy
Blanc Double de
    Coubert
Sally Holmes
Sea Foam
White Meidiland
Handel (pink edges)
Madame Alfred
    Carrière
Sombreuil
Honor
Crystalline
Double Delight (red
    edges)
Elina
Moonstone
Pristine
Whisper

French Lace
Iceberg
Nicole (red edges)
Gourmet Popcorn
Green Ice
Irresistible
Snow Bride

Purple/Mauve

Rose de Rescht
William Lobb
Hansa
Stainless Steel
Blueberry Hill
Purple Heart
Melody Parfumée
Incognito

Peach/Apricot

Abraham Darby
Evelyn
Felicia
Tamora
Royal Sunset
Westerland
Just Joey
Marilyn Monroe
Sunset Celebration
Amber Queen
Livin' Easy
Jean Keneally

Multi colored

Fourth of July
Betty Boop
Scentimental
Sheila's Perfume
Cherry Parfait
Hot Tamale
Magic Carrousel
Rainbow's End

White (Sombreuil)

Purple (Blueberry Hill)

Peach (Livin' Easy)

About This Guide

This book showcases 144 roses ideal for Northern California, divided into nine sections: species, old garden, modern shrub, groundcover, climbers and ramblers, hybrid tea, floribunda, grandiflora and miniature. Each section begins with an explanation of the characteristics of the class. The roses are arranged alphabetically according to their most common names. Alternative names are given below the main heading.

Clearly displayed in each entry are the features of the rose: the flowers' color, size and scent; height and spread ranges; bloom seasons and hardiness zones (see map, p. 8). Each entry contains information pertinent to growing and enjoying the rose.

The introduction to the book has tips for buying, planting, growing and caring for roses. The Glossary of Pests & Diseases beginning on p. 80 provides information on detecting and solving common problems.

Because our region is so diverse, we refer to seasons only in a general sense. Keep in mind the duration of seasons in your area when planning your rose garden. Hardiness zones can vary within a region; consult a local rose society, garden center or your county's University of California cooperative extension office for specific information. The resources section beginning on page 262 lists gardens, suppliers, offices for soil testing and rose societies in Northern California as well as books and websites about roses.

Blueberry Hill

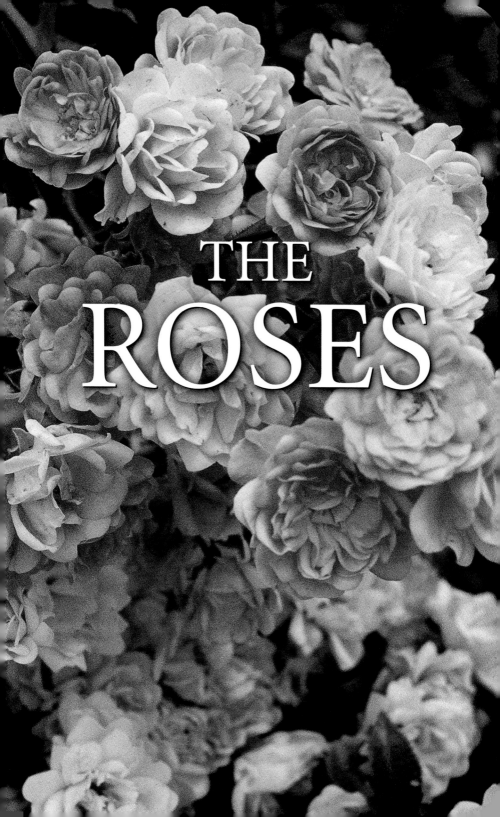

THE
ROSES

SPECIES ROSES

Species roses are roses that, when self-fertilized, produce seedlings that are identical to the parents. Species roses are very cold hardy and come in a variety of growth habits ranging from vigorous climbers to compact shrubs. Use species roses in informal borders, woodland gardens or hedges.

Species roses usually flower once a year and produce attractive hips. Some species roses have excellent fall color. This group of roses tends to be more resistant to drought and disease than modern roses. Unfortunately, species roses are not widely available, but the results are well worth the search.

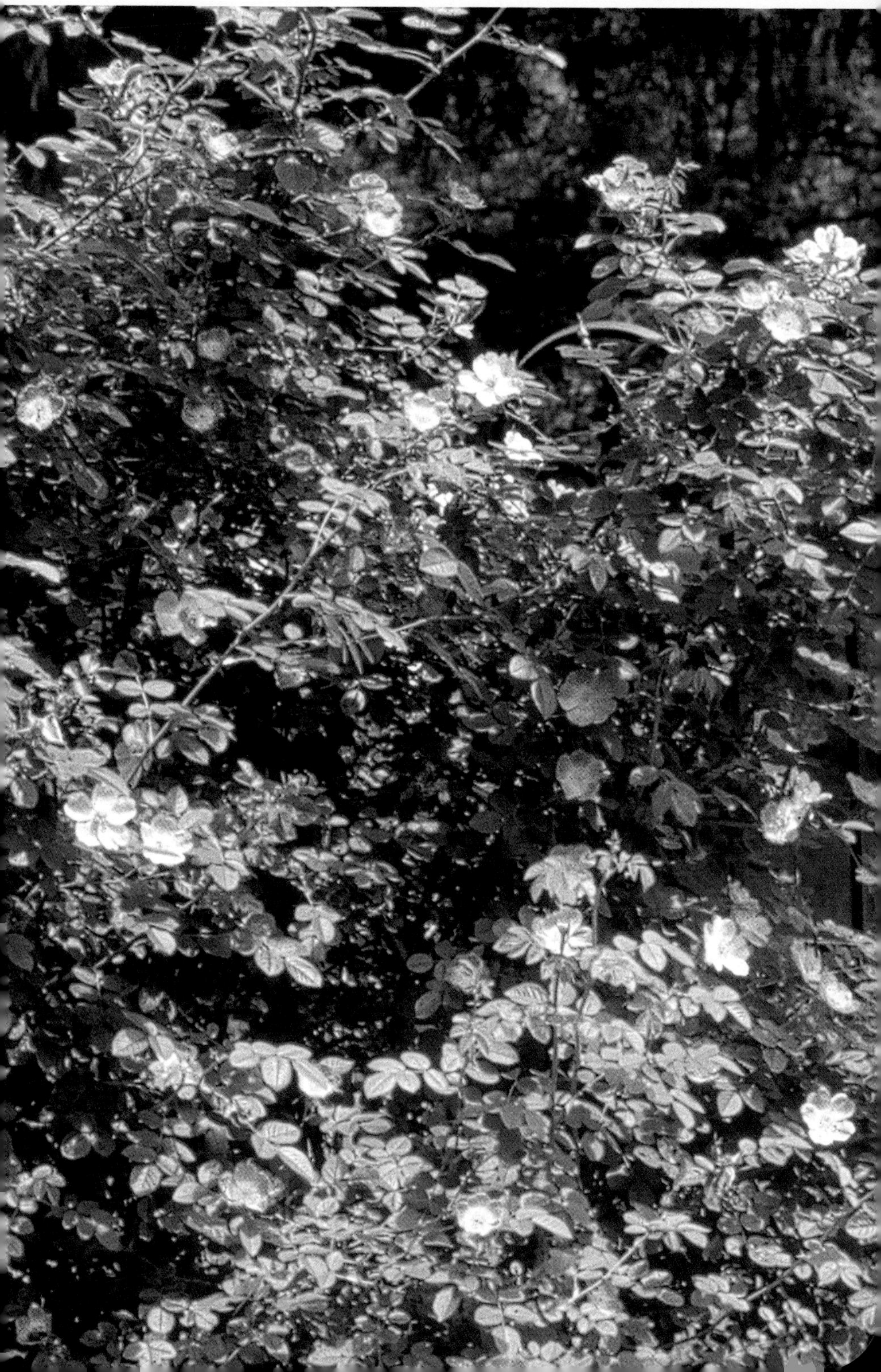

Rosa banksiae lutea

Other names:
Yellow Lady Banks Rose,
R. banksiae lutea plena
Flower color:
pastel yellow
Flower size: 3/4–1"
Scent: slight
Height: 25–30' or more
Spread: 25–30' or more
Blooms: early spring,
early summer; once-
blooming
Hardiness zones: 5–10

It is almost hard to believe your eyes when you first see a mature specimen of *R. banksiae lutea plena* left to its own devices. It has an abundance of blooms and its overwhelming stature gobbles up small buildings over time. You'd never know it by viewing an individual flower but this rose requires special care and attention if you don't want it to grow into a monster. The flowers are only part of the disguise. Small, double, pastel yellow flowers are produced along the long, wiry stems from top to bottom. Blooming only once per season, it bears a staggering amount of flowers over a six-week period beginning in very early spring. It was officially discovered in the 1820s but existed in a botanic garden in Calcutta, India, years before. This species rose deserves not only adoration but respect.

❀ Hardiest of the banksiae roses, it still prefers a warm and sunny climate. It requires little pruning but it's best to monitor it closely to prevent this rose from taking over small villages.

❀ The flowers are produced on second- or third-year wood. Growers have made astonishing claims about this species rose and one holds true: it not only holds its own with wisteria but also blooms at the same time, something that most other roses cannot do.

❀ The best place to plant *Rosa banksiae lutea* and leave it alone is at the base of an old tree or outbuilding. It can also be kept smaller with ardent pruning and discipline. Just be cautious of where you plant it, bearing in mind the stories of sheds collapsing under its weight.

Rosa eglanteria

During the 19th century, *Rosa eglanteria* was the preferred rootstock for grafting rose standards. Today it is still sought after since Carolus Linnaeus introduced it over 450 years ago. Those who know it love it, including Shakespeare who perfectly described this rose in 1594: '…a bank whereon the wild thyme blows, Where oxlips and the nodding violet grows/Quite over-canopied with luscious woodbine/With sweet musk-roses, and with eglantine.'

✿ Simple and wild in appearance, the foliage emits fragrance over and above the single, flat flowers. Glands located on the underside of the leaves produce a remarkable scent reminiscent of apples, especially on warm, early summer nights after a rain shower.

✿ This rose blends beautifully in locations including a woodland garden. It would be beautiful as a specimen or a dense hedge, where it could be kept in bounds with regular clipping. This practice may reduce the overall quantity of flowers but will encourage new aromatic shoots.

✿ Be sure to plant it away from areas with high traffic, as the canes are tremendously thorny. Ideally, it should be planted where the fragrance can be appreciated, such as under a window or near a sitting area.

✿ Rich red, oval hips often covered in fine bristles form after the flowers and remain on the plant well into fall.

Other names: Eglantine, *R. rubiginosa, R. suavifolia, R. walpoleana,* Sweet Briar Rose, Sweetbriar, Shakespeare's Rose, Shakespeare's Eglantine

Flower color: light pink

Flower size: 1½–2"

Scent: true rose

Height: 8–10'

Spread: 5–6'

Blooms: late spring to summer; no repeat blooming

Hardiness zones: 4–10

This trouble-free species rose should not be confused with Eglantyne, a modern English rose from David Austin.

Rosa glauca

Other names:
R. ferruginea, R. rubrifolia,
Red-leafed Rose
Flower color: pink;
white centers
Flower size: 1½"
Scent: little to none
Height: 6'; up to 12'
with support
Spread: 5–6'
Blooms: early spring to
mid-summer; no repeat
blooming
Hardiness zones: 2–9

*This rose received the
Royal Horticultural
Society Award of
Garden Merit, the offi-
cial stamp of approval
from the experts. It is
extremely popular
among rosarians and
novice gardeners.*

This rose thrives where most plants could not survive. It is used by municipalities in open planting
areas because it looks good and needs little care. The
starry, pink blossoms make a striking contrast to the
young violet-tinted foliage, which matures to a striking blue-gray. The flowers are followed by clusters of
small, rounded, dark red hips that remain on the
shrub well into the following spring.

✿ This species is sought by floral designers for its
colorful, dainty foliage, which is perfect for
arrangements. It is equally beautiful in the garden.
Rosa glauca is ideal for use as a hedge because of
its vigorous nature and arching, thorny, purple
stems. This rose has both looks and strength.

✿ *Rosa glauca* tolerates shade but prefers full sun,
which improves the depth of the foliage color.

✿ Regular pruning will regulate the plant size and
encourage new and colorful shoots.

✿ *Rosa glauca* was introduced into cultivation in
Britain before 1830. Its bushes can still be found
on the terrace at the Crathes Castle in Aberdeen,
Scotland.

Rosa virginiana

No serious rose lover's garden should be without *Rosa virginiana*. Its traditional form and reliable bloom make it a must for classical or cottage garden settings. It bears single, pink flowers in one large profusion in early summer. The flowers are sometimes mottled or a slightly deeper pink and expose long stamens. The gently serrated, glossy leaves are made up of seven to nine leaflets each.

Other names: Glossy Rose, Virginiana Rose
Flower color: medium pink
Flower size: 2–2½"
Scent: strong
Height: 5–7'
Spread: 3'
Blooms: spring to summer; no repeat blooming
Hardiness zones: 3–11

❀ The foliage changes from bright green to rich reds and yellows in fall. Shiny, bright red hips appear alongside the glowing fall foliage. The profusion of color is supported by reddish brown canes.

❀ The canes are often bristly with hooked thorns, making this species an ideal impenetrable hedge. It is also attractive in mixed beds and borders or as a specimen in a sunny location. It is a vigorous suckering rose, to the point of being almost invasive, so leave enough room for it to flourish.

❀ A white form, *Rosa virginiana* 'Alba,' performs in a similar manner but tends to be a little less showy.

OLD GARDEN

Old garden roses are those that were discovered or hybridized before 1867. Most bloom once during the growing season, producing a large quantity of fragrant flowers for a short time. Hybridizing in this class continued after 1867, but hybrids are still classified as old garden roses. This large and diverse class includes the following groups.

Gallica

Gallica roses are forms of *Rosa gallica*, often called the French Rose. It was the dominant rose from the 12th to the early 19th centuries but was in cultivation even longer. Many varieties and hybrids were discovered and propagated. These roses have upright, tidy to free-branching growth and intensely fragrant flowers that bloom once a year. The stems are moderately prickly, and fall foliage and hips are red. This hardy rose does not mind a little shade. Use gallicas in beds or borders, or as hedges or specimens.

Damask

Hybrids of *Rosa damascena*, damask roses are prickly, open, sprawling shrubs with intensely fragrant flowers. They have been cultivated for centuries for attar of roses, an expensive perfume and cosmetic base. Like the gallicas, damask roses played a role in the heredity of modern roses. There are two groups of damasks. Summer damasks, derived from crosses of *Rosa gallica* with *Rosa phoenicea*, bloom once a year. Autumn damasks, derived from crosses of *Rosa gallica* and *Rosa moschata*, bloom twice a year. Use damask roses in a border or train on a support. This group is hardier than most other old garden roses.

William Lobb

Alba

Alba roses are upright, graceful, free-branching shrubs with excellent pest and disease resistance, very good cold hardiness and good longevity. They are very low maintenance and bloom once a year with small clusters of small, intensely sweet flowers. Alba roses derive from a cross of *Rosa canina*, the dog rose, and *Rosa damascena*, the damask rose. They have been in cultivation since at least the time of the Roman Empire and were described by Pliny the Elder in his work *Historia Naturalis*. Alba roses are in the ancestry of many early hybrids. They are suitable for borders and beds, planted en masse or as specimens.

Centifolia

Centifolias, also known as cabbage roses, are very hardy, open shrubs with good pest and disease resistance and prickly stems. They are taller and more robust than gallicas. They bloom profusely with large, full, intensely fragrant flowers once a season. 'Centifolia' means '100-leaved,' referring here to the large number of tightly packed petals. Centifolias are derived from *Rosa centifolia*, likely a cross of an autumn damask and an alba cultivar. Use centifolia varieties in large borders or as specimens.

Moss

Moss roses began as sports of centifolia and damask roses. Balsam-scented, moss-like growth is produced on the flower buds, on the stems and sometimes on the foliage. The feel of the moss indicates the rose's origin—if a rose has supple, fern-like moss, it has been derived from a centifolia, while a rose with stiff, prickle-like moss has been derived from a damask. Moss roses are generally hardy to zone 6. They perform just as beautifully in colder regions and thrive from year to year with adequate winter protection and the right care and attention.

Mutabilis

China

China roses are compact, mostly smooth-stemmed, erect shrubs with an open habit. They tolerate high humidity, heat and drought. China roses are derived largely from *Rosa chinensis*, cultivated in China for centuries. They are not cold hardy but are highly disease resistant. There are few true China roses remaining in commerce because they have been replaced by newer cultivars that are hardier and, for some, more appealing. The flowers emit a fruity yet spicy fragrance that is refreshing but not overwhelming.

Portland

Portland roses are small, rounded, prickly shrubs with reasonable cold hardiness and a dislike of hot, humid climates. They are reliable repeat bloomers. Sometimes referred to as damask perpetuals, portlands derived from autumn damasks, gallicas and China roses. Their outstanding characteristics include a late flowering cycle and excellent red color. Hybridizers crossed the portlands with the everblooming China roses to produce the forerunners of the hybrid perpetuals. Use portland roses in the bed or border, or try them in a hedge.

Bourbon

Rosa borboniana, the first bourbon rose, was discovered on the Isle of Bourbon (now Reunion Isle, a small island in the Indian Ocean) in 1819 as a naturally occurring hybrid of China and autumn damask roses. Nearly all 19th-century hybridizers used this hybrid, and hundreds of cultivars were produced, with many of the best still widely available in commerce today. Bourbon roses are open, upright, vigorous shrubs with large, quartered flowers. They are mildly prone to blackspot and possess a variable level of cold hardiness. Use them in a border or bed, or train them on a fence, pillar, veranda railing or obelisk.

Hybrid Perpetual

Hybrid perpetuals are upright to free-branching, vigorous, prickly shrubs requiring winter protection in zone 6 or colder. This group is prone to fungal diseases in areas where the summers are very hot. Hybrid perpetuals are not truly perpetual as they do not bloom continuously, but they do bloom recurrently. They have a strong flush of blooms in spring, sporadic blooms through summer and a flush of blooms again in fall. The limited flower color ranges from pink to red to deep maroon. The foliage is generally disease resistant but susceptible to blackspot. This class has bourbon, portland and China roses in its ancestry and has virtually reached the end of its development, having no new introductions for at least 50 years. One hundred years ago this class was the dominant class for cut flowers and gardens, especially in colder regions where the tea roses were not hardy.

They are uncommon in commerce and highly valued by collectors.

Hybrid Spinosissimas
These roses are derived from *Rosa spinosissima* and are low-growing, suckering shrubs with fern-like foliage. They are very hardy and long lived, flowering profusely once a year in spring. The flowers are primarily single blooms in white, yellow or pink tones. The canes are heavily prickled although some varieties have few prickles. Many natural variations and hybrids have been introduced, but few remain in commerce. This group has been extensively used in gardens for hundreds of years. Occasionally new cultivars are introduced.

Noisette
Noisette roses, also called Champney roses, are vigorous climbing or sprawling roses. The first was discovered in South Carolina by John Champney and given to a nurseryman in France whose name was used for the class. Noisette roses derived from a cross between the China rose Parson's Pink China and *Rosa moschata*. Most cultivars were introduced in the 19th century, with a few remaining today. These roses are not cold hardy, and sustain damage when the temperature falls below freezing. They flower profusely in flushes from spring to fall, with up to 100 flowers per cluster. The heavy blooms have a tendency to weigh down the leggy canes, so support may be required. It is thought that this group introduced yellow and orange into the modern climbers. Also available in this class are dwarf roses suitable as bedding plants.

Charles de Mills

Tea Roses
Tea roses, or tea-scented China roses were collected by late 19th-century European explorers. Tea roses are upright, smooth to lightly prickly bushes or climbers derived from *Rosa* x *odorata*, a cross of *Rosa gigantea* and *Rosa chinensis* bred in China long ago, and should not be confused with modern hybrid teas. The fragrance resembles crushed tea leaves. The flowers are large and well formed but lack substance and strong canes. The teas provided the flower form, repeat-flowering habit and spicy fragrance to the hybrid tea class. They also passed along their intolerance of the cold. Historically tea roses were used in warm regions such as the southern US, but the hybrid teas are now more popular.

Charles de Mills

Other names: Bizarre Triomphant, Charles Mills, Charles Wills

Flower color: deep magenta pink

Flower size: 3½–5"

Scent: moderate to strong

Height: 4–5'

Spread: 3–5'

Blooms: spring to mid-summer; no repeat blooming

Hardiness zones: 4–9

Charles de Mills is the largest rose in its family. It is often in garden books as the perfect example of an old garden rose. The unusually large, purply pink blooms pack 200 petals or more into each flower. The flower color can be violet, crimson, wine, purple or maroon. The flat-topped buds, which open to flat blossoms and expose a green button eye in the center, make this a true gallica rose.

* The quartered blossoms are so full that the inner petals cluster and fold in toward the center. The petals look as if they have been clipped at the tips, resulting in puckered blooms, an unusual form.
* Under ideal conditions, this variety will become larger and bloom profusely. Its tolerance of poor soils and partial shade, however, makes it useful in just about any landscape setting, including mixed beds and hedging, and as an exhibition rose. It is also suitable for wild gardens, alongside meadows or larger gardens.
* The best location for this rose would be where its fragrance can be fully enjoyed—near a bench or under a window.
* Very little maintenance is required to keep Charles de Mills looking great. Remove old and unproductive wood once flowering is complete to encourage dense, lush growth and heavier flowering.

This rose is slightly prone to blackspot, so ensure its location has adequate air circulation. Mildew can also become a problem.

Fantin-Latour

Fantin-Latour, considered one of the most fragrant old garden roses, is officially classified as a centifolia but displays characteristics of other classes. It shares qualities with China and gallica roses, but not the repeat blooming. The flowers are produced in large clusters of flat, fully double, pale pink flowers, packed with 200 or more petals each. Each flower has a typical old rose button eye.

* The smooth, matte foliage tolerates hot and dry weather. It tolerates poorer soils and needs to be pruned after flowering to promote prolific blooming the following year.
* This fragrant and showy rose is used frequently as a large, spreading shrub. Once established, Fantin-Latour blends well into mixed beds and borders where space allows, and it is not troubled by larger tree roots. It grows even larger in cooler settings but can be pruned once the blooming is complete. When Fantin-Latour is supported and left unpruned, it can reach heights of 10'.
* Though centifolias are reputed to be prone to blackspot and to have unsightly flowers after rain, Fantin-Latour does not have these tendencies. This rose is moderately disease resistant but a little prone to mildew.

Other names: none
Flower color: pale pink
Flower size: 3–3½"
Scent: fresh, delicate and sweet
Height: 4–6'
Spread: 4–5'
Blooms: mid-spring to late summer; no repeat blooming
Hardiness zones: 5–9

It was named after the celebrated French painter Henri Fantin-Latour, known for his many still-life and old garden rose floral paintings.

Félicité Parmentier

Other names: Félicité
Flower color:
pale ivory pink
Flower size: 2½"
Scent: sweet and light
Height: 3–5'
Spread: 3–4'
Blooms: early summer;
no repeat blooming
Hardiness zones: 4–9

This rose received the Royal Horticultural Society Award of Garden Merit in 1993.

Considered one of the daintiest alba roses, Félicité Parmentier is an old rose said to date from before 1834 with origins unknown. Bearing classic, old-fashioned blooms, this rose only flowers once but for a long time. It grows into a dense and upright form. Certain characteristics resemble those of damask roses. Full ivory buds open to very double, quartered blossoms that emerge in clusters of three to seven in immaculate form. The flowers reflex after opening to form a perfect sphere of pale pink. The color fades to almost white over time and in hot weather.

❁ This rose is tolerant of poor soils and prefers to be planted in a partially shaded location.

❁ Like most albas, Félicité Parmentier has blue-gray foliage that resists fungal diseases, resulting in a disease-free specimen.

❁ Full flowers are supported by moderately thorny, stout stems. This old rose is ideal for cutting, arrangements and crafts.

❁ Félicité Parmentier is a vigorous, compact rose with a slight tendency to sprawl. It is useful for sunny locations with little room or more spacious spots in groups of three for impact. Cottage gardens that take you back to days gone by are the perfect location for this rose.

❁ Some rosarians think that Louis-Joseph-Ghislain Parmentier, a well-known Belgian nurseryman, is the breeder of this rose.

Harison's Yellow

This rose first appeared in attorney and amateur hybridist George F. Harison's garden in 1830, in the area now known as downtown Manhattan. It was carried by a number of pioneers on their journeys west and remains popular today. Harison's Yellow is one of the hardiest hybrid foetida roses in its class. It bears bright yellow, double flowers in a cupped form. Each flower is made up of 20 to 24 petals surrounding showy gold stamens. The sweetly scented flowers are known to hold their color until they fall away to the ground. It puts on a brief but spectacular show early in the season and is often the first rose to bloom in the spring. After blooming, the ferny foliage remains attractive while black bristly oval hips form and last well into the fall months.

Other names: Harisonii, *R. foetida harisonii, R. lutea hoggii, R. x harisonii,* Pioneer Rose, *R. x harisonii* 'Harison's Yellow,' *R. x harisonii* 'Yellow Rose of Texas'

Flower color: bright yellow

Flower size: 2–2½"

Scent: sweet and fruity

Height: 6–8'

Spread: 5–7'

Blooms: spring to summer; no repeat blooming

Hardiness zones: 4–9

❀ The blossoms occur along arching, mahogany canes with many prickles. Those canes form into an open but bushy shrub.

❀ Harison's Yellow tolerates drought, light shade and poor soils. It blooms more heavily in dry, cool locations.

❀ Known to spread quickly by suckers, it's easily propagated by planting the suckers separately as new plants. Or divide it like a perennial, with a shovel and a hatchet, to share with friends.

This rose received the RHS Award of Garden Merit in 1993.

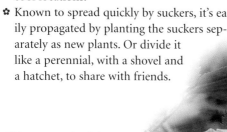
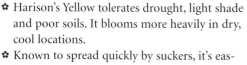

Jacques Cartier

Other names: Marchesa Boccella, Marquise Boçella, Marquise Boccella

Flower color: soft pink

Flower size: 4½–5"

Scent: rich and heady

Height: 3–4'

Spread: 24–36"

Blooms: spring to fall; repeat blooming

Hardiness zones: 5–9

Because there is no proof of the breeder or location and date of origin for this rose, some growers debate whether Jacques Cartier and Marchesa Boccella are the same rose. At rose shows, this variety is required to be called Marchesa Boccella, but it is typically known throughout North America as Jacques Cartier. Classification varies as well; it is regarded as a hybrid perpetual, a damask and a portland rose.

❀ The blooms display a green button eye surrounded by soft pink, double, quartered rosettes. The flowers emerge among leathery, light green foliage that changes over time to blue-green. Typical of portland roses, the small flower clusters of this variety huddle on the shorter stems. The flowers are slightly obscured within the foliage, giving the plant a neat and tidy appearance but reducing the overall impact of the blooms.

❀ It may be necessary to prune heavily or train horizontally to stimulate new, lush growth.

❀ Jacques Cartier resists disease and grows well in containers, as hedging and in mixed beds and borders. It prefers fertile, well-mulched soil.

❀ It was named after the 16th-century French master navigator who explored the St. Lawrence River and searched for a Northwest Passage.

Louise Odier

L ouise Odier is one of the most floriferous old garden roses available in commerce. It is considered a first-rate cut flower and has long been popular among those who love roses. It grows into a bushy, upright but arching framework that supports camellia-like blossoms held on long stems. Soft olive green leaves and maroon prickles cover the stems. Each well-formed, fully double flower is the perfect shape for a bourbon rose, cupped at first then opening flat and round, sometimes quartered, with central petals touched with lavender. The flowers are continuously produced, without fail, from the middle of summer to fall frost.

Other names:
Mme. de Stella

Flower color: medium pink with a hint of lavender

Flower size: 3½–4½"

Scent: rich and sweet

Height: 4–5'

Spread: 4'

Blooms: mid-summer to fall; repeat blooming

Hardiness zones: 5–10

❀ Louise Odier is best grown with support. It tolerates dappled shade and with winter protection it can withstand zone 4.

❀ If left unpruned, it can be trained as a climber, but more often it is used as a valuable addition to a mixed border.

❀ Even with a lower petal count, the blossoms are very full. The rather slender, upright growth habit is not typical of the big, flowing bourbon roses yet it seems to fit well into its classification.

Raised by Margottin in 1851, this rose is the parent of many popular French roses.

Madame Hardy

Other names: none

Flower color: white

Flower size: 3–3½"

Scent: fresh and sweet with a hint of citrus

Height: 4–5'

Spread: 3–5'

Blooms: mid-spring to mid-summer; no repeat blooming

Hardiness zones: 4–9

Madame Hardy tolerates poor soil and light shade but tends to be less prolific under these conditions. In full sun, it will flower profusely for three to four weeks.

Give it everything it requires, and Madame Hardy will produce the most perfect white flowers you could imagine. This rose bears hundreds of large, flat, double, green-eyed, white blossoms. The emerging flowers sometimes display a hint of pale pink when they first open, and the blooms are set against densely packed, lush, matte green foliage. Each flower is made up of 150 to 200 petals that almost totally obscure the stamens.

❧ Once Madame Hardy is established, it is very easy to grow in mixed borders, beds and cut-flower gardens or as a specimen.

❧ Every three years or so, prune the plant down to 1–2', just as the long shoots are beginning to get out of control. Remove the older wood down to the crown.

❧ This rose is extremely resistant to blackspot but highly susceptible to mildew. Hot sun immediately after a substantial rainfall can cause the leaves to develop small blotches.

❧ Since its 1832 introduction, Madame Hardy has been praised for its fragrance, and it received acclaim as the most beautiful white rose in the world. Alexandre Hardy, chief horticulturist of Paris' Luxembourg Castle, created this and many other rose varieties; he named this one after his beloved wife.

Mutabilis

Mutabilis flowers look like butterflies perched among the leaves. This rose bears vermilion buds that open to buff yellow, single flowers. The flowers then turn various shades of pink and finally a deep shade of crimson. It is common to see this flowering shrub in a state of constant change similar to the color changes typical of wild China roses, from which this rose likely came. Each single flower is made up of an average of five velvety petals. The changing color palette is an unusual but desirable trait that would brighten even the gloomiest site.

Other names:
Tipo Idéale, *R. chinensis mutabilis, R. odorata 'Mutabilis,'* Butterfly Rose

Flower color: yellow, then pink and crimson

Flower size: 2–3"

Scent: little to none

Height: 4–6'

Spread: 3–5'

Blooms: mid-spring to mid-summer; repeat blooming

Hardiness zones: 5–10

* This variety has been known since 1896 but was not introduced officially until 1932 when a Swiss botanist, Henri Correvon of Geneva, received it from Prince Ghilberto Borromeo's garden. No one knows where it originated or whether it occurred naturally.
* This rose could be used to climb up the side of a house, cover outbuildings or as a large specimen. The size and shape will vary depending on the location. Some claim that this rose can reach heights of 10–25' when it is left alone on a sturdy support.
* Soft, red stems support the glossy, red-tinged dark green foliage, which is impervious to disease. This rose requires very little maintenance. It tolerates shade but is not fond of cold winds.
* The name is Latin for 'changing,' possibly a reference to the changing color of the petals.

Reine des Violettes

Other names:
Queen of the Violets

Flower color: magenta
with touch of lavender

Flower size: 3"

Scent: sweet, heady,
peppery

Height: 3–5'

Spread: 3–5'

Blooms: early spring
to fall; repeat blooming

Hardiness zones: 6–9

The blooms of Reine des Violettes are close to a true blue. The flowers open carmine purple and turn violet mauve. The color is most striking later in the season, as the days become cooler and shorter. The abundant gray-green, smooth, peppery-scented foliage blends well with the color of the flowers. It is reminiscent of a gallica bloom in shape and color, but some say it more closely resembles a bourbon rose. Classified as a hybrid perpetual, Reine des Violettes has an intoxicating fragrance.

❀ This rose is somewhat susceptible to blackspot but more disease resistant than any other hybrid perpetual. Fungal problems are easily alleviated by proper watering practices (see Watering in the book's introduction).

❀ Reine des Violettes is a heavy feeder. Regular but careful pruning diminishes a leggy and sparse growth habit, and a hard pruning every three to four years will encourage a more solid form.

❀ Full sun, rich, well-drained soil and good air circulation are the only essentials for the success of this variety.

Rose de Rescht

A number of theories have arisen over the years about where this rose came from and when and how it was discovered. Some experts have stated that it originated in Iran while others think it was found in a garden in France. The most popular explanation is that an English gardener named Nancy Lindsay brought Rose de Rescht from Persia to England in the 1940s. Whatever its origins, this rose produces intensely fragrant, deep purple roses with a vibrant hue in just about any climate. Each double blossom has at least 100 petals in a camellia-like form. The flowers sometimes appear a little ragged but its rich aroma is reason enough to plant this rose.

Other names: Rose De Rescht, Gul e Rescht

Flower color: deep vibrant purple

Flower size: 2–2½"

Scent: sweet, heady

Height: 2½–3½'

Spread: 2–3'

Blooms: summer to fall; repeat blooming

Hardiness zones: 4–9

✿ Easy to grow and receptive to a hard pruning, this rose is ideal for planting en masse or within a mixed border.

✿ Some damask roses, including this one, repeat bloom and are often called autumn damask roses.

✿ The colorful flowers are known to pale in the hot sun but last for long periods. The flowers repeat in six-week intervals from summer to fall.

✿ Rose de Rescht is healthy and durable, tolerates poor conditions and requires little care.

Rescht is an ancient caravan town in modern-day Iran.

Stanwell Perpetual

Other names: none
Flower color:
pale pink, almost white
Flower size: 3–3½"
Scent: classic tea
Height: 3–5'
Spread: 4–6'
Blooms: late spring
to fall; repeat blooming
Hardiness zones: 3–9

Stanwell Perpetual has an uncertain history. Some say that it was developed by one of the two—Lee and Kennedy—who marketed the rose in 1838. It was happened upon in a garden at Stanwell in England. When it was released, it was classified as a hybrid spinosissima. It is also known as a burnet cross. Regardless of the controversy and mystery, it can bear 100 or more blooms in one flush, which completely obscure the grayish green foliage. The quartered flowers have an average of 45 to 55 petals each. The color intensifies as the temperatures cool in late summer. The double flowers have muddled centers and frilled edges. The fragrant flowers are followed by only an occasional red hip. Each cane is well clothed in long, reddish prickles and light foliage touched with purple.

✿ Pruning is unnecessary, but removing old canes to the ground yearly will encourage flowers to grow. Don't be surprised to see this rose sucker. Prune out unruly growth when necessary.
✿ This beauty tolerates just about anything, including poor soil, drought, drenching rain, intense summers and hard winters. It is resistant to most disease but mildly prone to blackspot.
✿ Ideally suited to mass plantings in exposed areas and slopes, it is also stunning as a flowering border or impenetrable hedge.
✿ The foliage emits a subtle, sweet aroma when wet with rain or morning dew.

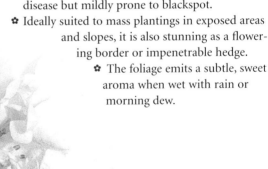

William Lobb

William Lobb is very popular and the most vigorous of all moss roses. The buds and sepals at the base of the flower clusters are covered in moss and smell of pine, especially when touched. Upright, arching, bristly canes form an open growth habit with coarse, large, dark gray-green leaves.

Other names: Duchesse d'Istrie, Old Velvet Moss

Flower color: dark crimson purple

Flower size: 3"

Scent: very sweet

Height: 6–8'

Spread: 5–6'

Blooms: mid-spring to mid-summer; no repeat blooming

Hardiness zones: 4–9

❀ The base is sparsely leafed, so plant another flowering shrub or perennial in front to disguise this characteristic.

❀ Hard pruning after flowering will create a more stout form but still showcase the unique grayish brown moss and prickles. It can grow very large in zones 5 through 7. The long stems require support when climbing pillars, tripods, pergolas, walls, trellises, arbors and arches.

❀ This rose, bred by Laffay in France in 1855, was named after the plant huntsman who brought the Monkey Puzzle Tree from Chile and popularized it in England.

MODERN SHRUB

The category of shrub roses comprises a variety of rose groups. Shrub roses are easy to grow and generally very hardy. They can be compact or quite large and often have prickly stems. The newer varieties bloom continuously and have good pest and disease resistance. The following groups fall into this category.

English Roses

Roses in this small but expanding group were bred by David Austin Roses Ltd. and first became prominent in the 1970s. Although the flowers display the classic antiquity of old garden roses, they are modern roses, with the positive qualities of a newer generation, including improved disease resistance. The foliage is moderately prone to blackspot. They are specifically chosen for their flower form, reliable growth

habit, foliage and fragrance. They are ideal for cutting. The canes of English roses are not as robust as those of the hybrid teas, and often the large, beautiful flowers nod at the top of the canes. English roses generally need protection from cold winters.

Hybrid Musk Roses

Hybrid musks are a result of crossing *Rosa multiflora* with noisette varieties. Hybrid musks are very adaptable to climate. They do not mind the heat of the south and are hardy in all but the cold-est parts of Northern California. Protection during extremely cold winters is recommended. They are mostly recurrent bloomers and the flowers have a trademark musky tea scent.

Polyantha Roses

Polyantha roses were derived by Jean Baptiste Guillot, who crossed the climbing variety *R. multiflora* and the repeat-flowering China Old Blush. Polyantha blossoms emerge in sprays well above their foliage. The small to tiny flowers are produced in large clusters, and the

The Fairy

flowers often completely cover the plant. Polyanthas were crossed with hybrid teas to produce floribundas

Rugosas

This group contains a large number of varieties and hybrids of *Rosa rugosa*, a widespread, hardy rose with wrinkled, disease-resistant foliage. It is easy to identify hybrids that have *Rosa rugosa* as a parent. Rugosas are good, tough roses for the landscape, providing interest all year. They have naturalized in many areas near the ocean. They bloom in spring and fall, have attractive foliage and produce large orange-red hips that provide color through late fall and winter. They respond well to heavy pruning but should not be sprayed with any type of chemical because the foliage is easily burned. They are suitable for beds, borders and hedges and as specimens. Because they tolerate salt, rugosas can be used near roads, sidewalks, pathways and driveways.

Shrub Roses

Shrub roses exhibit an elegant form unlike other rose bushes. Whereas most modern bushes are bred for their ability to repeat flower, shrubs are suitable for just about any garden setting. Not only are shrub roses easy to grow, but many varieties take on a naturally graceful form. Although the majority of shrub roses in commerce bloom throughout the summer, some blossom only once.

Sally Holmes

Mary Rose

Abraham Darby

Other names: Abraham, Country Abraham, Country Darby

Flower color: apricot yellow tinted with pink

Flower size: 4–5"

Scent: strong and fruity

Height: 5–6'

Spread: 5'

Blooms: early spring to late fall; repeat blooming

Hardiness zones: 5–9

When cut in bud, the long-lasting flowers are wonderful for arrangements.

Abraham Darby is one of the most widely grown roses developed by David Austin Roses Ltd., and justifiably so. It has a strong growth habit, fruity fragrance, old-fashioned flowers and a reliable repeat bloom. It is moderately disease resistant and extremely vigorous.

✿ This rose, named after one of the prominent figures of the Industrial Revolution, bears small clusters of large, double blooms on well-armed, arching stems with waxy, dark green leaves.

✿ With its flexible canes, this rose can be trained as a climber. It is also ideal for borders or as a specimen when left in its natural form. Place it where the fragrance can be fully appreciated.

✿ Prune only to remove dead or diseased wood and to help shape the bush into a well-formed, bushy, mounded shrub. It blooms well on new wood so can be pruned more if needed.

✿ It thrives in good weather and is prone to blackspot. The flowers are known to ball when wet.

Ballerina

Ballerina was raised by Reverend Joseph Hardwick Pemberton and introduced by his gardener, John A. Bentall, in 1937. Reverend Pemberton was a distinguished English rosarian, exhibitor, president of the Royal National Rose Society and originator of the hybrid musk rose. After the reverend died, Bentall bred his own hybrid musk creations. Ballerina falls into several classifications including polyantha, hybrid musk and modern shrub. It bears large, cascading clusters of single, dainty flowers. The lightly speckled flowers emerge a soft pink with a pale reverse and well-defined pink edges. The pink fades to a pinkish white eye at the base of the petals surrounding the golden stamens.

Other names: none

Flower color: pinkish white; darker pink edges

Flower size: 1–2"

Scent: subtle musk or sweet pea

Height: 3–4'

Spread: 4'

Blooms: mid-spring to early summer; repeat blooming

Hardiness zones: 4–9

❀ The flowers are supported by a dense mass of small, semi-glossy leaves on almost thornless stems. Tiny orange-red hips follow the flowers in fall.

❀ Ballerina is relatively trouble free and resistant to most disease. It tolerates light shade and poor soil. The flowers may need deadheading after the first flush to keep the plant from looking tired.

❀ With its arching growth habit, this rose could work as a weeping standard. It is suitable for hedging, mixed borders, containers and mass groupings. It can also be trained as a climber on a trellis or fence.

The flowers have been compared to apple blossoms, but this rose was given its name because the blooms resemble a ballerina's skirt.

Blanc Double de Coubert

Every rose garden should include one of these magnificent rugosas. Along with its dazzling white blooms, this rose has an interesting history and outstanding reputation. It was introduced in 1892 in France; Coubert is the French village where its creator lived. It bears leathery, wrinkled, dark green leaves. Loose-petaled, semi-double clusters of white, fragrant flowers are borne from buds occasionally flushed with a hint of pink. Each flower is made up of an average of 15 to 25 petals.

Other names: Blanche Double de Coubert, Blanc de Coubert
Flower color: crisp white with yellow stamens
Flower size: 3"
Scent: strong and sweet
Height: 5–7'
Spread: 4–5'
Blooms: spring to fall; repeat blooming
Hardiness zones: 3–9

❀ Moderately vigorous, this arching, dense shrub tolerates light shade and most soils. It is highly resistant to disease.

❀ The soft-textured petals are easily marked and affected by rain, so they might appear spent not long after opening.

❀ Deadheading after the first flush will encourage more blooms. Stop deadheading closer to fall so that hips will develop. The hips transform into reddish orange spheres that stand out among the stunning fall foliage.

❀ Blanc Double de Coubert is excellent for hedging, borders or specimens. The blossoms are ideal for cutting, but cut the stems when the blooms are still partially closed to extend the flowers' vase life.

Bonica

A Meilland introduction in 1982, Bonica was the first modern shrub rose to be named an All-America Rose Selection when it received that honor in 1987. It is durable and highly recommended for mixed beds, containers, hedges, cut-flower gardens or as a groundcover, standard or specimen. It bears an abundance of rich, semi-glossy foliage. The blooms are lightly scented. Bright orange hips follow the double pink rosettes through winter.

✿ Easy to maintain, this rose tolerates most conditions including shade and poor soils. It is disease resistant and hardy.

✿ Bonica is a tidy, sprawling rose of modest size that blooms profusely through most of the growing season. It is suitable for just about any location.

✿ It's not surprising that this beautiful rose has been popular throughout the world since its introduction.

Other names: Bonica '82, Meidomonac, Demon, Bonica Meidiland

Flower color: medium pink

Flower size: 1–2"

Scent: sweet and delicate

Height: 3–5'

Spread: 3–4'

Blooms: spring to fall; repeat blooming

Hardiness zones: 4–9

Buff Beauty

Other names: none

Flower color:
rich apricot yellow

Flower size: 3"

Scent: sweet tea,
tropical fruit, musk

Height: 5–6'

Spread: 5–6'

Blooms: mid-spring
to late summer; repeat
blooming

Hardiness zones: 4–9

Over the years there has been a little controversy regarding the parentage and breeder of Buff Beauty. Some claim that Pemberton developed this hybrid musk in 1922. Others say that Bentall or his widow created it in 1939. Regardless, this variety is not only useful but beautiful as well. It bears sprays of small, double, apricot yellow flowers. The colorful blooms contrast beautifully with the coppery plum foliage that matures to a deep, dark green. The flowers fade to a creamy buff over time.

❀ Buff Beauty tolerates less fertile soils and partial shade. It withstands poor weather and continues to bloom profusely until fall.

❀ The long stems make this a good choice for a cutting rose. It is also suitable for hedging when plants are placed close together. It can be trained as a small climber on low fences and pillars.

❀ Buff Beauty is striking when mixed with a variety of colorful plants or left alone to show off in its own container.

❀ This rose is vigorous and dense, exhibits a spreading tendency, yet is strong and self supporting. It will perform with very little care.

With its unique flower color and handsome foliage, this rose is almost a collectible, ideal for the rose enthusiast.

Carefree Wonder

The versatile Carefree Wonder lives up to its name as an outstanding, all-around landscape rose. Municipalities throughout North America use this variety in public areas. It is considered an everblooming variety, bearing flowers continuously throughout summer and fall with a reliable repeat bloom. Each bloom has 25 to 30 bright pink petals with a lighter reverse. The cupped form exposes a white eye that surrounds the vivid yellow stamens. The bright pink tones deepen in cooler weather. As the blooms age and respond to temperature change, they create a mosaic of pink hues, ranging from hot pink to soft pink.

Other names: Dynastie, Carefully Wonder
Flower color: bright pink blend
Flower size: 4–5"
Scent: subtle
Height: 4–6'
Spread: 3–5'
Blooms: spring to fall; repeat blooming
Hardiness zones: 3–9

✿ This rose is easily distinguished by its heavily and deeply serrated foliage and reddish bristles. Bright reddish brown hips begin to form in fall, an indication that winter is just around the corner.

✿ Carefree Wonder is great for foundation plantings, informal hedging or as a self-contained shrub. It is very effective when planted en masse or as an accent. The arching growth habit and a little training would make this rose a fantastic groundcover in a larger garden setting.

✿ Few cluster-flowered roses exhibit all their positive qualities as beautifully or as long as Carefree Wonder. As its name implies, it is low maintenance, resistant to disease and highly recommended. It received the prestigious AARS designation in 1991.

Deadheading after the first flush encourages a faster repeat of flowers.

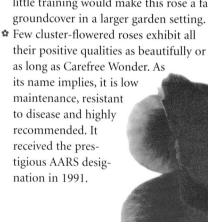

China Doll

Other names: none

Flower color: medium pink with hints of yellow at each petal's base

Flower size: 1–2"

Scent: light tea

Height: 2'

Spread: 2'

Blooms: spring to fall; repeat blooming

Hardiness zones: 4–9

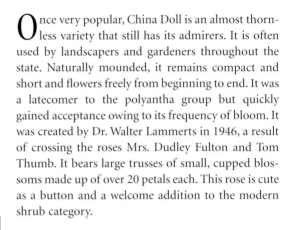

Once very popular, China Doll is an almost thornless variety that still has its admirers. It is often used by landscapers and gardeners throughout the state. Naturally mounded, it remains compact and short and flowers freely from beginning to end. It was a latecomer to the polyantha group but quickly gained acceptance owing to its frequency of bloom. It was created by Dr. Walter Lammerts in 1946, a result of crossing the roses Mrs. Dudley Fulton and Tom Thumb. It bears large trusses of small, cupped blossoms made up of over 20 petals each. This rose is cute as a button and a welcome addition to the modern shrub category.

* The delicate-looking flowers provide a constant display throughout the growing season. Profuse blooms are one of China Doll's many outstanding characteristics.
* China Doll's low-growing habit makes it an ideal low border or short standard. It's also very effective when planted en masse.
* The leathery leaflets are clean and rarely affected by disease.
* Also available is a climbing China Doll, which has similar characteristics but can grow much taller. It is also very effective in brick planters and hanging baskets.

Evelyn

When Evelyn was released in 1992, its breeder, David Austin, stated that it had the strongest, most delicious scent of all the Austin roses. Members of the Canadian Rose Society voted Evelyn the sixth most popular fragrant rose. The complex scent of this rose contains up to 84 different chemicals. Evelyn has other special characteristics as well. It bears huge, fully double, shallow-cupped rosettes in shades of pale apricot. The blooms are muddled in the centers, showcasing the yellow base of each petal. The satiny petals intertwine within, creating a beautiful form unlike that of any other rose. The apricot shades can change in hotter weather, a characteristic inherited from one of its ancestors. Evelyn gets its vigor and yellow color from Graham Thomas and its apricot pink color from Tamora.

Other names: Apricot Parfait

Flower color: soft blend of apricot, pink and yellow

Flower size: 3–4"

Scent: sweet and fruity

Height: 3–4'

Spread: 30–36"

Blooms: early summer to fall; repeat blooming

Hardiness zones: 5–9

Crabtree and Evelyn, a famous English company known for a range of rose-scented products, chose Evelyn to represent its perfumes in advertising and packaging.

- Evelyn forms into a upright, bushy, medium-sized shrub. It blooms profusely and continuously through the season, and is ideal for mixed shrub and perennial borders. In warm climates it can grow taller and may require support.
- It thrives with little to no pruning. The foliage is healthy but a little prone to blackspot. Try to avoid wetting the foliage. Water only at the base of the shrub, early in the morning.
- Evelyn is a fantastic cut-flower rose. The fragrance of one cluster can fill an entire room. Its vase life is longer than that of most roses.
- It may not be the most vigorous of the Austin roses, but its profusion of flowers is reason enough to integrate this rose into any garden setting.

Felicia

Other names: none
Flower color:
blush peach
Flower size: 2–3"
Scent: sweet and
fairly strong
Height: 5'
Spread: 5'
Blooms: spring to fall;
repeat blooming
Hardiness zones: 4–9

*Felicia makes a spec-
tacular cluster-flowered
shrub when pruned
hard in early spring.
Lighter pruning creates
a symmetrical specimen.*

Felicia bears a profuse show of apricot buds that open to a blush peach. The flowers pale to off-white as they age, more frequently in spring and fall. This rose blooms sporadically throughout summer and produces mounds of glossy foliage among large panicles of long-lasting flowers well into late fall.

✿ Felicia is suitable for cutting, hedging, containers, mixed borders and beds. It is best suited to partial shade and is highly resistant to disease.

✿ Felicia requires deadheading to promote further blooming, but leave some flowers on the plant so hips can develop at the end of the growing season. The late hips will also signal the plant that winter is just around the corner. Eventually the hips turn deep red and remain on the shrub until the following spring.

✿ This rose is considered one of the best of its class. It won the National Rose Society Certificate of Merit in 1927 and the Royal Horticultural Society Award of Garden Merit in 1993.

Frau Dagmar Hastrup

Frau Dagmar Hastrup is one of the most compact rugosas, ideal for a smaller garden. It is sturdy and vigorous with a spreading habit and strong disease resistance. Pale, silvery pink, shallow-cupped flowers are followed by huge, tomato-shaped, dark red hips. Wrinkled leathery foliage covers the prickly gray canes.

- Frau Dagmar Hastrup is used widely in natural woodland settings, shrub borders, low ground-cover hedges or in front of larger-growing species roses or flowering shrubs.
- This low-maintenance rose tolerates a little shade to full exposure.
- This variety resists disease but may experience dieback in harsh winters. It will re-shoot.
- A small thicket of stocky suckers will form when the bud union is planted below ground level. Make sure you plant it at the correct level.
- The foliage changes from maroon to deep russet gold in fall. Along with the showy hips, this rose adds outstanding color to a fall setting when other plants are about to finish.
- Frau Dagmar Hastrup was originally released as a 1914 introduction from Denmark. It won the Royal Horticultural Society Award of Garden Merit in 1993.

Other names: Frau Dagmar Hartopp
Flower color: light silvery pink
Flower size: 3½–4"
Scent: strong cinnamon and cloves
Height: 3–4'
Spread: 4'
Blooms: spring to fall; repeat blooming
Hardiness zones: 2–9

Bees love this rose; if you want to attract them to a sunny vegetable garden, plant this rose nearby.

Golden Celebration

David Austin roses are famous for their scent, and Golden Celebration is no exception. Austin described the blooms of this rose as tea scented but with a combination of sauterne wine and strawberry. The flowers' fruity scent is strong enough to catch the attention of someone walking by. Ovoid buds emerge in spring and open to densely packed, deep cups of golden yellow petals. These intricate flowers have slightly recessed centers and an old-fashioned appearance. The rounded, colorful flowers perch themselves beautifully atop the thick, flexible canes clothed in dark, glossy foliage.

Other names: none
Flower color: golden yellow
Flower size: 5–6"
Scent: strong, fruity, tea-like
Height: 5–6'
Spread: 5–6'
Blooms: spring to fall; repeat blooming
Hardiness zones: 5–9

❀ Golden Celebration is a reliable rose that is easy to grow in just about any circumstance. It works well in borders or left alone as a colorful specimen. With pruning and training Golden Celebration can either be a medium-sized shrub or a short climber. Its shapely growth habit eventually forms into a beautifully rounded shrub on its own, suitable for any garden setting.

❀ This 1992 introduction has an old-fashioned appearance but not an old-fashioned color. It would be beautiful in a mixed rose border or planted en masse for impact.

❀ The long, arching stems are easily bowed down during wet weather.

Golden Celebration is considered one of the largest-flowered and most stunning Austin roses ever developed.

Golden Wings

Golden Wings has set the standard for single-flowered yellow shrub roses since its 1956 introduction. It is a living memorial of its creator, Roy Shepherd, a famous rosarian who died in 1962. It bears delicately ruffled, soft yellow flowers that emerge long before most other roses and bloom continuously throughout the season. The cupped flowers consist of an average of five to seven petals that open into large saucers with prominent amber stamens. Each cluster is followed in fall by uniquely shaped green hips. It vigorously produces strong, prickly stems covered with clear, light green leaves.

❀ Deadhead to extend the blooming season. It is best to prune Golden Wings back substantially to reduce the possibility of straggly growth.

❀ This rose tolerates poor or less fertile soils and partial shade. The foliage is highly disease resistant but more prone to blackspot along the coast.

❀ Use this variety in mixed borders or hedges. It is considered one of the best landscape roses available. It provides structure within a wide border and is effective as a specimen when left alone.

❀ Without adequate winter protection in colder areas, this variety may experience severe dieback, or die completely.

Other names: none
Flower color: medium yellow
Flower size: 4–5"
Scent: subtle orange and honey
Height: 4½–5½'
Spread: 4½'
Blooms: spring to fall; repeat blooming
Hardiness zones: 4–9

Graham Thomas

Other names: English Yellow, Graham Stuart Thomas

Flower color: deep butter yellow

Flower size: 4–5"

Scent: strong, old-fashioned tea

Height: 5–8'

Spread: 5–6'

Blooms: early spring to fall; repeat blooming

Hardiness zones: 5b–9

Its narrow, upright growth habit makes this rose a good standard.

Graham Thomas was developed in 1983 by David Austin Roses Ltd. as the first true yellow English rose. It was named after one of the most influential rosarians of our time. It bears beautiful apricot-pink buds that open into large golden yellow blooms. The double blooms carry up to 35 petals and fade gracefully in time. The flowers remain cupped until the petals fall cleanly from the plant. This rose is very dense and upright in form, bearing an abundance of light green leaves.

✿ In warmer climates this extremely vigorous rose will grow taller if supported, developing into a pillar style or climbing rose. A light pruning will allow Graham Thomas to remain a little smaller if desired, but this rose may remain naturally small in cooler climates.

✿ Long, flexible stems often flop under the weight of the beautiful but short-lived flowers.

✿ Deadheading may be required to extend the prolific blooming cycle.

✿ Wet weather will not trouble this rose, but excessive heat may cause reduced flowering, blackspot and fading flower color.

✿ Graham Thomas received the Royal Horticultural Society Award of Garden Merit in 1993.

Hansa

Hansa, first introduced in 1905, is one of the most durable, long-lived, fragrant and versatile roses. Hansa specimens have been found blooming near buildings abandoned for decades. It bears deeply veined, leathery foliage on arching, thorny canes. Large, double, loose clusters of dark mauve-red blooms make this rose showy enough for mixed borders and beds, hedges or specimens. Spectacular foliage and large, orange-red hips follow in fall.

Other names: Hansen's
Flower color: mauve purple
Flower size: 3–3½"
Scent: strong, cloves
Height: 4–7'
Spread: 5–6'
Blooms: spring to fall; repeat blooming
Hardiness zones: 3–9

✿ Canes five years old and older may need pruning to improve the vigorous flower production, which will naturally decline with age.

✿ It thrives in silty clay to sandy soils, freezing weather, salt air and wind. It tolerates hard pruning and poor conditions but dislikes alkaline soils.

✿ In milder climates the plant might become leggy and the flower color may fade. Pruning regularly can correct the growth habit.

✿ Like most rugosas, Hansa tolerates neglect and still flowers profusely throughout the season.

Heritage

Other names: Roberta
Flower color:
pale blush pink
Flower size: 4–5"
Scent: sweet with
lemon undertones
Height: 6–6½'
Spread: 5–6'
Blooms: spring to fall;
repeat blooming
Hardiness zones: 4–9

*The graceful flowers
do not lend them-
selves to cutting and
are better left to
adorn the garden
instead of your house.
The flowers are very
short-lived and fragile,
though easily
replaced.*

Though bred in 1984, Heritage has the appearance, scent and overall performance of an old
English garden rose, and its name is a nod to that
heritage. In this blend of new and old, the strengths
outweigh the weaknesses. Heritage is a nicely formed
shrub with virtually thornless canes that support
semi-glossy, smooth, dark green foliage. The breeder,
David Austin, considered this the most beautiful
English rose he ever created, with its double sprays of
medium-sized, clear pink blooms. The center of each
flower is a soft and clear pink while the outer petals
are almost white. This isn't just another pink rose—
its alluring scent is reminiscent of tea with a touch of
honey and lemon.

✿ Heritage performs best in fertile, well-mulched
   soil in mixed borders, hedges and beds.
✿ This rose is moderately resistant to disease; take
   the proper measures to prevent mildew and
   blackspot, including watering at the base rather
   than from overhead.
✿ Some rose growers have said that Heritage blooms
   in sparse and sporadic waves when young, but
   we've experienced profuse blooming and overall vigorous growth in the first year. The
   blooming only increases over time, resulting
   in a prolific flowering shrub suitable for any
   garden setting.

Lavender Lassie

Lavender Lassie is a versatile rose that tolerates most soil and light conditions. It is valued as one of the few lavender-colored repeat-blooming shrubs. The blossoms open flat to jumbled centers, similar to the form of an old-fashioned rose. Though one of its parents was a hybrid musk, Lavender Lassie tends to behave more like a cluster-flowered rose. It grows into a strong, freely branched shrub bearing an abundance of semi-glossy foliage.

* The large clusters are very weighty and dense enough to pull the branches down to the ground.
* Lavender Lassie is widely used because it is highly disease resistant and has an upright, vigorous nature. It tolerates poor soil and a little shade without the flower color suffering.
* In warmer regions the long canes can be trained to crawl up fences, walls or pillars. When left alone, Lavender Lassie is suitable as a specimen or planted in mixed beds or shrub borders.

Other names: none
Flower color: medium pink with lavender
Flower size: 3"
Scent: strong, lilacs
Height: 5–7'
Spread: 4–5'
Blooms: spring to fall; repeat blooming
Hardiness zones: 4–9

Linda Campbell

Other names: Tall Poppy
Flower color: medium red with a lighter reverse, yellow stamens
Flower size: 3"
Scent: slight to none
Height: 6–8'
Spread: 6–8'
Blooms: spring to fall; repeat blooming
Hardiness zones: 4–10

Linda Campbell was considered a breakthrough in rugosa breeding in the early 1990s. No other rugosa hybrid with such bright red coloring and sheer volume of blooms existed at the time. Created by Ralph Moore of miniature rose fame and introduced in 1991 in the US, it was named in honor of a rosarian and former editor of the *American Rose Annual*. Linda Campbell is the offspring of a hybrid rugosa and a miniature rose. It has very dense rugosa-like growth and bears medium-sized, fiery red flowers that repeat very quickly. Considering its rugosa parentage, it's relatively thorn free and a great low-maintenance specimen or hedging plant.

✿ Semi-double flowers consist of 25 petals each in a cupped form. The color fades slightly over time but remains vibrant to the last moment before the petals fall to the ground. The flowers occur in large clusters of 5 to 20 blooms on the tip of each arching cane.

✿ Hardy to zone 4, this rose requires little care or maintenance owing to its parentage and tolerance of extreme temperatures.

✿ It is also known to thrive in the heat, and in fact prefers it. Neither cold nor heat is a match for this rose.

✿ A mile-long stretch of Linda Campbell roses has been planted along a road between Fresno and Hanford. These stunning roses are hard to miss.

Mary Rose

Mary Rose is one of the most bountiful and hardy of the Austin English roses. Its medium pink flowers, touched with lavender, darken with age. The bloom cycle is long, readily replacing one double, lightly fragrant flower after another. The blooms are borne at the tips of prickly, arching stems covered in emerald green, matte foliage.

✿ Mary Rose is a great all-around shrub, ideal for group plantings, hedging and mixed borders. The classic, loose-petaled blooms mix well with a variety of other plants.

✿ This variety is not good for cutting because the blooms are fragile and can shatter before they fully open.

✿ Mary Rose and its two sports are strong, disease resistant and tolerant of most soils and exposures. Its two sports are Winchester Cathedral, which bears pure white, fragrant flowers, and Redouté, a lighter pink rose.

✿ With its uneven growth habit, this rose may need to be reshaped with light pruning from one year to the next. Deadheading encourages further blooming.

✿ This variety was introduced in 1983 and is named after Henry VIII's flagship, which was recovered from the Solent River in England 400 years after it sank.

Other names: none
Flower color: medium pink
Flower size: 4–4½"
Scent: sweet honey and almonds
Height: 4–6'
Spread: 5'
Blooms: early spring to fall; repeat blooming
Hardiness zones: 5–9

Outta the Blue

Other names: none

Flower color: magenta to lavender blue with yellow in the center

Flower size: 1½–2"

Scent: sweet, spicy, clove and rose

Height: 2'

Spread: 2'

Blooms: spring to fall; repeat blooming

Hardiness zones: 4–9

Outta the Blue is a Tom Carruth creation, introduced in 2002. This modern shrub is part of the Modern Antique series by Weeks Roses. They are new, modern roses that resemble old varieties but have better disease resistance and overall health. It vigorously produces double flowers with 25 to 30 petals each. The purple shades turn different hues in different climates. They're borne in large clusters in an old-fashioned form.

❧ The most outstanding feature of this rose is its subtle color changes throughout the season. The fragrant flowers change from one purple-pink hue to the next, always evolving into another magical color.

❧ Outta the Blue grows to be a medium upright plant with a slightly rounded form. It requires little pruning or care to maintain its shape.

❧ It was the result of crossing Stephen's Big Purple, International Herald Tribune and a *R. soulieana* derivative.

Pat Austin

Pat Austin is a modern English shrub rose introduced in 2002 by David Austin Roses Ltd. It is named in honor of Austin's wife, Pat, an accomplished sculptor. It introduced a new vivid color combination to the English rose series: rich copper shades on the uppersides of the petals and pale amber yellow on the undersides. Semi-glossy, deep green foliage complements the large, open, deeply cupped, coppery flowers. The growth is strong and slightly arching. It would be difficult to miss the exceptional contrasting tones as the strongly fragrant flowers open and expand.

Other names: none
Flower color: coppery amber and yellow
Flower size: 2½–3½"
Scent: fruity and sharp
Height: 3'
Spread: 4'
Blooms: spring to fall; repeat blooming
Hardiness zones: 5–9

✿ Pat Austin is an ideal medium-sized shrub. It can also be trained to become a short climber. It blends beautifully into mixed shrub borders, informal beds or containers.

✿ With its unique color, high level of disease resistance, graceful spreading form and strong and vigorous growth habit, this rose will likely become extremely popular.

✿ As a recent introduction, Pat Austin may be difficult to find, but it is well worth looking for.

Prospero

Prospero is perfect for those who prefer the purple shades that are rarely found outside the gallica class. It is has flowers with perfect symmetry in a slightly domed rosette shape. The large, fully double flowers have pointed petals in rich crimson tones that turn more purple with age. The deep tones are even darker toward the center owing to the 100 or so clustered petals. The result is a rose that resembles antique varieties of royal stature. Then there's its wonderful scent. It's no wonder people fall in love with English roses.

Other names: none

Flower color: crimson to purple

Flower size: 3–4"

Scent: intense, fruity

Height: 2–3'

Spread: 2–3'

Blooms: repeat blooming; spring to fall

Hardiness zones: 5–9

✿ Prospero is most successful in a warm, dry climate. It creates the most impact in a border, short hedge, container or small garden setting.

✿ Considered by some to be a challenge, even David Austin himself claims this rose is less than robust. When contented, however, its blossoms are hard to beat and fragrance is second to none.

✿ The name comes from Shakespeare's play *The Tempest*.

Sally Holmes

S ally Holmes bears large trusses of single, creamy white flowers lightly touched with peach. The flowers fade over time until they are almost pure white when fully open. The clusters are enormous, each stem carrying 50 or more blooms on graceful arching canes. Some people claim that the clusters are too close together, but while they may seem a little cluttered, they are stunning. Each flower is made up of five petals that open flat to expose prominent stamens. The flowers are complemented by large, semi-glossy, pointed leaves.

❀ It's easy to be impressed by the magnificent flowers, but this rose's most beautiful feature is its balance. No one characteristic outshines the others, and all the features work together to create a beautiful package.

❀ This rose thrives in full sun but tolerates partial shade. Deadhead early in the season to prolong the blooming cycle.

❀ The petals will fall cleanly from each stem, resulting in a well-formed hip.

❀ This highly disease-resistant rose is easily trained as a climber along a fence or wall in warmer locations. It is effective as a specimen and blends well with various other flowering plants in mixed beds and borders.

Other names: none
Flower color: creamy white with peach undertones
Flower size: 3½"
Scent: light, sweet
Height: 3–5'
Spread: 3–5'
Blooms: spring to fall; repeat blooming
Hardiness zones: 4–9

Tamora

Other names: none
Flower color:
apricot blend
Flower size: 3–4"
Scent: sharp, lilac
Height: 3'
Spread: 3'
Blooms: spring to fall;
repeat blooming
Hardiness zones: 4–9

Tamora has a bewitching scent, reminiscent of myrrh and spice.

Another beauty created by David Austin, Tamora is an earlier variety that is especially popular in warmer climates where it remains smaller in stature. It is closely related to old Gloire de Dijon and has inherited both its coloring and fragrance. It bears glorious pale apricot flowers touched with hints of soft pink. The reddish orange buds unfurl into large blossoms. Forty silky petals, layered in an old-fashioned style, appear darker at the center and pale toward the edge. The petals part slightly, creating a shallow cup in the center. It exhibits each and every wonderful quality of an English rose.

❀ The best flower color and size is most evident in cooler weather.
❀ Tamora vigorously spreads and matures below the height of an average shrub rose. It is suitable for beds, borders and hedges because of its contained growth and well-balanced form.
❀ The name Tamora comes from a character in a Shakespearean play called *Titus Andronicus*.
❀ Tamora was the result of crossing Chaucer with Conrad Ferdinand Meyer, and was introduced by David Austin Roses in 1983.

The Fairy

The Fairy is trouble free and highly resistant to disease, requiring very little care. It is popular with both novice and experienced gardeners. The moderately thorny canes are hidden by glossy foliage that forms into a compact and mounding form. It bears dainty, baby pink rosettes that develop into large clusters perched atop the leaves.

Other names:
Fairy, Feerie
Flower color: soft pink
Flower size: 1–1½"
Scent: very little to light
Height: 24"
Spread: 2–4'
Blooms: late spring to late fall; repeat blooming
Hardiness zones: 4–9

✿ Pruning may be necessary to maintain The Fairy as a dwarf shrub. When left in its natural form, it grows into a delicate, spreading shrub. With light pruning, it can spread to almost 7' wide on the coast but remains slightly more compact in the interior.

✿ This rose is ideal for a variety of landscape purposes. It can be planted in a container or as a groundcover or left to trail over a low wall or embankment. It is easily trained as a weeping standard and integrates nicely into mixed beds and borders. It packs a punch when planted en masse or as low hedging. It also makes a beautiful cut flower.

✿ This rose blooms continually until fall frost or a forced dormancy.

✿ The Fairy doesn't just tolerate neglect, it prefers it. It manages successfully in partial shade, and the shade slows the fading of the flower color.

The Mayflower

Other names:
The Mayflower Rose,
Mayflower

Flower color: deep pink

Flower size: 3–3½"

Scent: strong, old rose
fragrance

Height: 3–4'

Spread: 3'

Blooms: spring to fall;
repeat blooming

Hardiness zones: 5–9

The Mayflower is a very recent introduction from David Austin Roses, available in this country since 2003. It represents an important new breakthrough in English roses. It appears to be free of any disease and completely resistant to blackspot, powdery mildew and rust based on a number of long-term trials completed in England, Europe and the US over a nine-year period. It grows into a small shrub bearing blossoms reminiscent of old roses in deep, crisp shades of pink. This variety has a unique blooming cycle as it never produces a great mass of flowers at any one time but flowers with regularity seldom found in any other rose. It forms into a bushy and unusually full, twiggy bush with small matte green foliage, and it is rarely without flowers.

❀ The Mayflower is ideal planted at the front of borders, en masse and in containers.

❀ This variety is touted as the toughest David Austin rose to date.

❀ The Mayflower was named to mark the opening of a new David Austin Rose Garden at Matterhorn Nurseries, north of New York City.

Thérèse Bugnet

Thérèse Bugnet is a little hesitant to bloom when young but it's well worth the wait. Once established or when it is at least two to three years of age, it will produce smooth, gray-green leaves on almost thornless canes. The stems are tipped with a profusion of ruffled, double, lilac pink blossoms that pale with age. After the flowers have all but finished, attractive fall colors prevail, with cherry red canes, orange hips and bronze foliage creating a distinctly beautiful shrub.

Other names:
Theresa Bugnet

Flower color: medium lilac pink

Flower size: 3–4"

Scent: sweet cloves

Height: 5–6'

Spread: 5–6'

Blooms: spring to fall; repeat blooming

Hardiness zones: 2–9

✿ This exceptional rugosa variety tolerates cold and heat, wind and late frosts. Thérèse Bugnet doesn't mind partial shade to full sun, alkaline, rocky, sandy or clay soils or neglect.

✿ One of the cold-hardiest roses in the world, this variety endures temperatures of −35° F.

✿ Like other rugosas, Thérèse Bugnet resents being sprayed with fungicides. If mildew occurs, prune out and destroy infected growth.

✿ Deadheading regularly and pruning after the first flowering cycle in early summer will prolong the blooming cycle. Otherwise, the only pruning required would be to cut the magnificent flowers for arrangements.

✿ This rose blooms sparsely on the coast; some rose growers believe it needs colder winter temperatures to bloom.

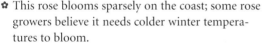

GROUNDCOVER

These roses are not groundcovers in the true sense of the word but are a good addition to large areas that need color. Generally groundcover roses remain small and have a procumbent or spreading habit. The best groundcover roses grow wider than taller, repeat bloom throughout the summer without deadheading, are disease resistant and require minimal winter protection. Groundcover roses can reach heights of 3–4'. Their compact and floriferous growth habit provides a mass of dense foliage and color. Often groundcover roses send down roots where the canes touch the ground. Some hardy, low-growing hybrids have been developed recently that work very well as groundcovers. Smaller, hardy roses can also be mass planted to fill a large area with color.

Most groundcover roses benefit from a hard pruning in spring and extra mulching in late fall. Use once-a-year fertilizers in spring if the roses are planted in areas that are difficult to access.

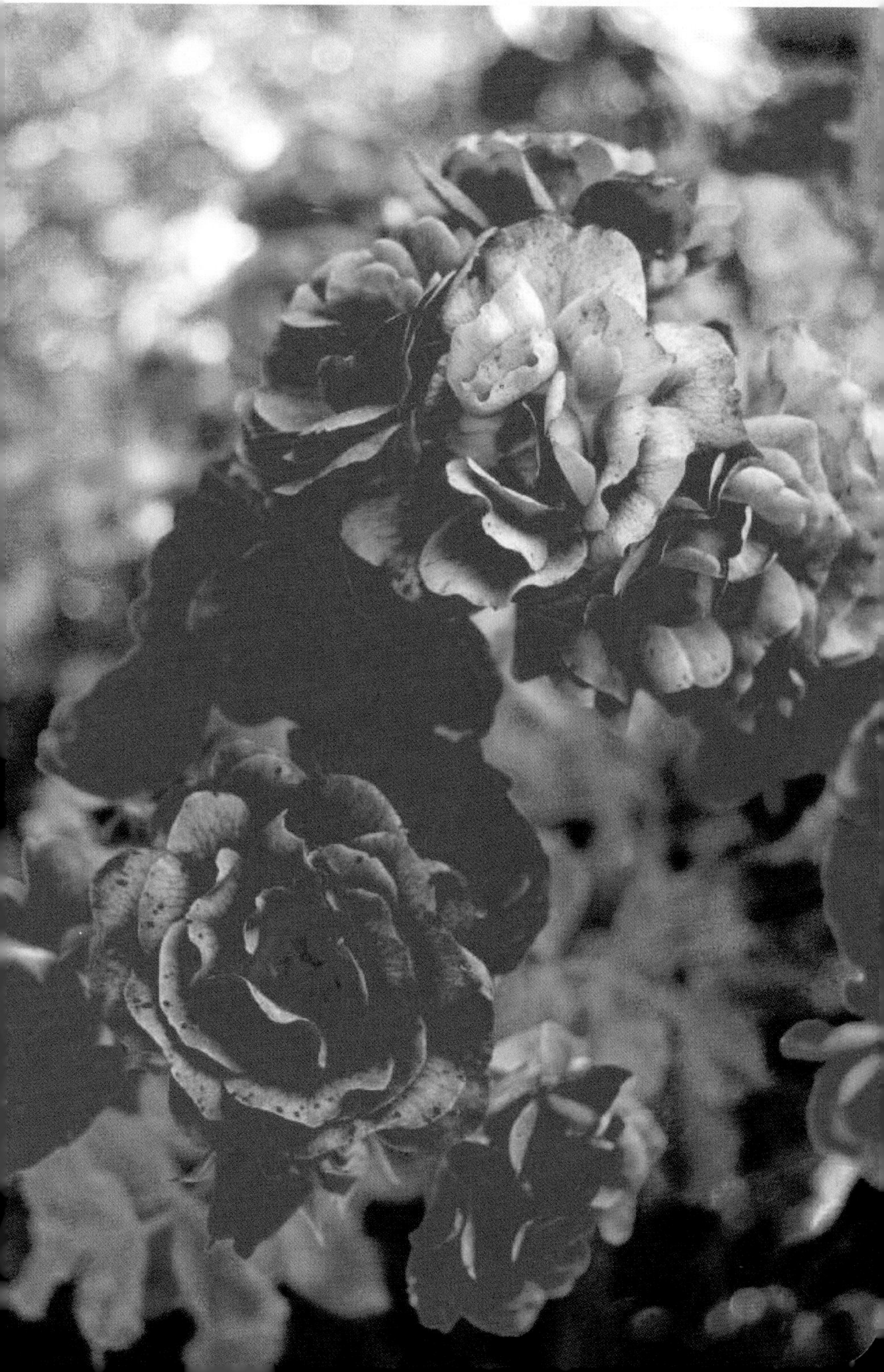

Baby Blanket

Baby Blanket is a low-growing rose that is trouble free and constantly in bloom. It appears dainty but displays rugged characteristics. Baby Blanket was a breakthrough in low-maintenance gardening when it was introduced in 1991 by W. Kordes Söhne Roses of Germany. It bears double, light pink flowers made up of 20 to 25 petals each. The flowers are borne in large clusters and mildly fragrant. They stand above dark, glossy foliage that is as tough as nails.

❀ Baby Blanket produces canes with an arching habit that allows it to be trained as a small rambling rose. Knee-deep mounds of foliage are ideal for use as groundcover. It's also suitable left as a specimen. It is available as a short tree or standard rose for areas that require a vertical lift, but it may need some winter protection.

❀ This rose requires very little care other than the basics. Baby Blanket is not only pretty but practical in every sense.

❀ Plant Baby Blanket roses in front of taller Bonica (p. 125) roses for a striking combination.

Other names: Oxfordshire, Sommermorgen, Summer Morning, Country Lass

Flower color: light pink

Flower size: 2–3"

Scent: slight

Height: 2–3'

Spread: 5'

Blooms: summer to fall; repeat blooming

Hardiness zones: 4–9

Ferdy

Ferdy is often grown as a low-growing ground-cover because of its spreading growth habit. It is a little taller than the average groundcover rose but spreads to twice its height. The blossoms are small and nearly scentless but plentiful. Masses of blooms are borne in clusters that almost completely obscure the foliage underneath. Each flower is double in form and consists of 20 deep pink petals. An abundance of matte foliage supports the copious flowers all season long.

Other names: Ferdi
Flower color: deep salmon pink
Flower size: 2–3"
Scent: little to none
Height: 3'
Spread: 5–6'
Blooms: summer to fall; repeat blooming
Hardiness zones: 5–9

✿ Blooms are produced on small laterals along the canes of the previous season's growth. It shouldn't be pruned in winter for this reason.
✿ The flowers are known to fade and remain on the bush for lengthy periods.
✿ Because of the lack of repeat bloom, deadheading is crucial to ensure blooming cycle longevity and to remove the flowers once they're spent.
✿ Ferdy's cascading growth makes it an ideal weeping rose when grafted onto taller standard stock, where it can arch gracefully down to the ground.
✿ Ferdy was bred by Seizo Suzuki of Japan in 1984.

Flower Carpet

Other names: Heidetraum, Emera, Emeura, Blooming Carpet, Emera Pavement, Pink Flower Carpet, Floral Carpet

Flower color: deep hot pink

Flower size: 2"

Scent: very little

Height: 24–32"

Spread: 3–3¹/₂'

Blooms: summer to early winter; repeat blooming

Hardiness zones: 5–9

Flower Carpet was developed in 1991 and proclaimed to offer 'flowers for 10 months' and 'total disease resistance.' The claims proved a little too optimistic, but this variety is still beautiful and multifaceted. Vigorous, shiny, plentiful foliage complements the double, hot pink flowers. The blooms are borne in large clusters with bright yellow stamens, creating a dense, colorful carpet of flowers, hence the name. This rose can survive winters in zone 4 with winter protection.

✿ Thanks to its rambler parentage, its prolific flowering begins a little later than most other roses, and at times there are no blooms at all. A good hard winter prune every year will restore the vigor of any Flower Carpet plant that has become too woody. Cut it down to 10–12" above ground at that time, removing any old wood.

✿ Deadheading isn't necessary because the petals fall cleanly from the plant while it continues to bloom.

✿ Flower Carpet can be used as a groundcover for a sunny location or as a low hedge. It can also be used in containers, hanging baskets, mixed borders or beds.

✿ This plant has reliable disease resistance, but blackspot may occur in humid climates, especially if it becomes wet later in the day.

✿ A new color of Flower Carpet has been introduced almost every year since its original release, including white and a variety of pink shades. Watch for Appleblossom, White, Pink, Red, Coral and Yellow, the color introduced in 2004.

Nozomi

Nozomi has an exquisite trailing habit that stretches five feet but only grows over a foot tall. This modern climbing miniature rose is frequently used as a groundcover or climber. The tiny, single flowers are borne on the previous years' wood so little pruning is required. The flowers emerge as tiny buds that open into light pink, starry-shaped blossoms that lighten to pearl pink. The flowers are borne in trusses amid small glossy foliage. It was created by Onodera from Japan in 1968. Nozomi means 'hope' and was the name of the breeder's niece.

✿ This mound-forming rose will root into the ground where the stems make contact with the soil. It is only necessary to prune the old stems in winter to maintain the low-growing habit.

✿ Nozomi makes a fine weeping standard when grafted onto taller rose stock. It is also very effective when displayed in a container.

✿ This rose is tolerant to a little shade and will grow successfully in poor soil.

✿ Nozomi is a little prone to blackspot but generally resistant to disease.

Other names:
Heideröslein Nozomi
Flower color: light pink to white
Flower size: 1"
Scent: little to none
Height: 12–18"
Spread: 5'
Blooms: mid-summer to fall; repeat blooming
Hardiness zones: 5–10

Ralph's Creeper

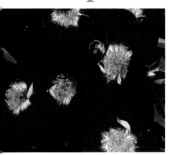

Ralph's Creeper is another prostrate growing rose that remains low to the ground and produces small but dense and healthy growth. It is particularly vigorous for a shrub and can be grown on slopes to prevent erosion, in window boxes for a trailing effect or in an area that requires coverage. It's a fine choice for those who want to cover the ground with dense matte foliage and red flowers with bright yellow-white eyes. Each flower is made up of 15 to 18 petals.

Other names: Creepy, Glowing Carpet, Highveld Sun, Trailing Red

Flower color: dark red with a bright yellow reverse and a yellow eye

Flower size: 2¹/₂–3'

Scent: moderate, apple blossom

Height: 18–24"

Spread: 5'

Blooms: spring to fall; repeat blooming

Hardiness zones: 4–9

✿ The flowers open almost flat in a semi-double, loosely cupped form. Sprays of 10 to 15 flowers each contrast beautifully with the dark foliage and thorny stems.

✿ It requires little care and attention and will even tolerate shade.

✿ Ralph's Creeper is a self-cleaning rose: the petals will fall cleanly from the stem once spent. A round orange-red fruit or hip will begin to form after the petals fall.

✿ It was named in honor of Ralph Moore, the American miniature rose hybridizer who created this beauty. He is currently in his mid-90s and continues to produce masterpieces as he has for decades. This rose was introduced in 1987 and to this day Mr. Moore states that Ralph's Creeper is not a miniature variety but a shrub with climbing miniature and floribunda parentage.

Red Ribbons

R ed Ribbons is an ideal groundcover rose for difficult locations. Naturally vigorous, low spreading and dense in growth habit, this rose is ideal for cascading down embankments, growing up short pillars or planted en masse. The semi-double to double, dark red flowers stand out in any landscape setting. It is well recognized around the world for its hardiness, charm and versatility. It can also be found as a grafted standard or tree rose.

Other names: Fiery Sunsation, Chilterns, Mainaufeuer, Island Fire

Flower color: bright, deep red

Flower size: 3"

Scent: mild

Height: 2'

Spread: 4–5'

Blooms: summer to fall; repeat blooming

Hardiness zones: 4–9

✿ Like so many roses bred by Kordes, Red Ribbons is winter hardy and produces healthy foliage.

✿ Don't confuse Red Ribbons with Red Ribbon, a floribunda introduced in 1997 by J. Benjamin Williams. Both roses bear double red flowers but have different parentage, breeders and countries of origin.

✿ Red Ribbons is part of a collection of low groundcover roses called Rose Blanket roses, introduced in the US by Jackson & Perkins. Other members of this group include Baby Blanket, Electric Blanket and Magic Blanket.

Sea Foam

Other names: Seafoam
Flower color: white touched with pink
Flower size: 2–2½"
Scent: delicate tea
Height: 2–3'
Spread: 4–6'
Blooms: summer to fall; repeat blooming
Hardiness zones: 4–11

Sea Foam falls under several classifications. It is a modern shrub rose with a climbing or rambling habit, and it is often used as a groundcover rose. Abundant clusters of pale pink buds emerge in summer, a little later than other roses, and open to attractive pearly white blossoms. Sea Foam is rarely without its beautiful double, cupped flowers. The flowers are supported by moderately thorny canes clothed in dark, leathery foliage.

✿ The spreading habit causes it to grow out and downwards rather than up. It is easily trained as a groundcover rose trailing down an embankment or stone wall. It can also be trained as a short climber with adequate winter protection.

✿ The plant will root on its own wherever its flexible canes contact the ground. It is easily propagated by cuttings or by layering.

✿ Sea Foam prefers full sun but continues to thrive in partial shade. The pink tones will intensify in cooler settings or partial shade.

✿ This rose was developed by an amateur hybridizer, Ernest W. Schwartz, in 1964. It shouldn't be confused with another rose called Seafoam, which was bred in 1919 by William Paul and is said to be a seedling of Mermaid.

White Meidiland

Two roses within the Meidiland series are often confused. Both are white and very similar in appearance, but differ in subtle ways. White Meidiland bears a larger flower and grows only a fraction as tall as its counterpart Alba Meidiland. The flowers are very double and made up of 40 petals each, overlapping to form a large, 4" wide blossom. White Meidiland's bloom period is slightly different than that of Alba Meidiland, as it bears flowers in prolific flushes from late spring to fall. White Meidiland is largely disease free, which is why this rose is so ideally suited for use along roads, borders and gardens that receive little care.

✤ The spreading growth and vigorous horizontal branching makes it ideal for use as a groundcover. It was originally released for this purpose simply because of its procumbent growth habit, density, prolific blooming and ease of care.
✤ White Meidiland does not drop its petals cleanly. It will require deadheading to keep it looking tidy.
✤ Mrs. Marie-Louise Meilland developed White Meidiland in 1986 for Meilland Roses of France. It is officially registered with the ARS under the code name MEIcoublan; Alba Meidiland is registered as MEIflopan.

Other names: Alba Meidiland, Blanc Meillandecor
Flower color: pure white
Flower size: 3–4"
Scent: sweet
Height: 1½–2'
Spread: 4–5'
Blooms: summer to fall; repeat blooming
Hardiness zones: 4–9

CLIMBERS & RAMBLERS

Climbing roses do not in fact climb. The canes must be trained and tied in place on some form of support. Climbers generally have long, stiff, arching canes ranging in length from 8–15'. The canes are productive for more than two seasons and often become thick and woody.

Climbing roses come from various sources, and the hardiness of a variety depends on its parentage. For just about any climate or region, there is a climber, including climbing hybrid teas and climbing Explorer series roses. Pruning practices can greatly influence the form of your climbing rose. Vigorous shrubs can be pruned to encourage upright growth, and climbers can be pruned to resemble shrubs.

Hybrid teas, floribundas, grandifloras and other bush or shrub roses sometimes mutate to produce long, vigorous canes, referred to as 'sports.' Climbing sports produce the same flower types and blooming habits as the roses they sported from. Some seedlings are grown and propagated as a source of climbers. The more recent introductions are less rampant than the older types and are repeat blooming. The canes terminate in an inflorescence, later flowering from laterals produced on the main canes.

Ramblers have longer, flexible canes that can reach lengths of 20' or more. Rambler canes behave like raspberry canes in that new canes grow without

flowering for their first season, and flowers are produced along the canes in the second season. When the flowering cycle is complete, the canes should be pruned out. Ramblers need to be tied to a support when trained to grow in an upright direction. They can also be left to 'ramble' along the ground or to trail down an embankment or stone wall.

Early climbers and ramblers arose from crossing hybrid teas and other classes mainly with *Rosa wichuraiana* and *Rosa multiflora*. They bloomed once a year and were often rampant growers. *Rosa wichuraiana* is an ancestor of many modern climbers, and there are still many non-repeat Wichuraiana climbers available in commerce.

Albertine

Albertine is an aggressive rambler suitable for covering a fence, pergola or the side of a house. It is also effective as an unsupported specimen shrub. Its reddish buds open to delicate, salmon pink blooms with an average of 25 petals each. The clusters of richly scented flowers are borne on the tips of plum-colored, arching branches. Striking, glossy purplish green foliage fills out to create a dense form.

✿ It flowers for approximately three to four weeks in mid-summer.
✿ The stems may require repeated securing as the plant reaches its mature height and spread.
✿ Generally disease resistant, Albertine is a little prone to mildew in drier climates and seasons.

This rambler is revered for its outstanding fragrance and profusion of blooms.

Other names: none
Flower color: salmon pink
Flower size: 3"
Scent: richly fragrant
Height: 15–20'
Spread: 15'
Blooms: mid-spring to mid-summer; no repeat blooming
Hardiness zones: 5–9

Altissimo

Altissimo is Italian for 'in the highest.' It is an apt name for this high climber, which is also highly disease resistant. Large, matte, leathery, dark, serrated foliage complements the nearly flat, deeply colored flowers. The large blooms are borne on new and old growth. Altissimo is considered one of the best red climbers and one of the easiest climbers to grow. The single flowers almost obscure the plant throughout the season.

❀ Remove the spent blooms to encourage long-term, prolific blooming. The nearly rounded, blood red petals sometimes fall off soon after the large, single flowers have opened.

❀ When cut, the blooms retain their color and are useful in a variety of arrangements.

❀ In a warm location, Altissimo has been known to grow large enough to cover the side of a one-story building. In a cooler location, it doesn't grow as large.

❀ This rose can be grown successfully as a large shrub if pruned hard and given room to fill out. If trained as a climber, it will require support on a pillar, pergola, veranda post or trellis. The stiff and sturdy stems create an upright, bushy and spreading form suitable for just about any garden setting.

❀ George Delbard of Delbard-Chabert developed this stately climber in 1966 in France. Altissimo is a seedling of Tenor, a red climber also created by Delbard.

Other names: Altus, Sublimely Single
Flower color: crisp, blood red
Flower size: 5"
Scent: slight
Height: 10–14'
Spread: 8'
Blooms: early spring to mid-summer; repeat blooming
Hardiness zones: 4–9

America

Other names: none
Flower color: deep salmon pink with lighter reverse
Flower size: 3$\frac{1}{2}$–4$\frac{1}{2}$"
Scent: intense, spicy
Height: 7–8'
Spread: 4–6'
Blooms: summer to fall; repeat blooming
Hardiness zones: 5–9

America can tolerate being pruned to maintain a large, manageable shrub.

This large-flowered climber bears deep salmon pink flowers with a lighter reverse. Intensely spicy blossoms are borne singly and in clusters amidst medium green, semi-glossy foliage. Famed hybridizer William A. Warriner of Jackson & Perkins created this rose in 1976. In the year of its introduction, America was chosen as an AARS winner. It is one of the very few climbers to receive such a prestigious distinction. It flowers freely throughout the summer months on old and new wood. The flowers are deeper and more vibrant immediately after opening but they fade over time to a pale coral salmon. Each flower is very double, made up of 40 to 45 petals with a high center in a cupped form.

✿ This climber performs best in a protected location. Exposure to winter conditions will damage its canes and limit its height. With winter protection, America can withstand zone 4 and 5 temperatures.
✿ It is excellent for cutting and suitable for climbing walls, fences and pillars.
✿ Deadheading is recommended to boost repeat blooming cycles throughout the summer months until fall.
✿ This rose was introduced in the year of the bicentennial celebration of the United States.

American Pillar

Despite its name, American Pillar is considered too aggressive to be a pillar rose and is better suited to climb up the side of a house, pergola, wire fence or lattice, or to twine around an old, sturdy tree. It bears large clusters of small, deep pink flowers with prominent yellow stamens. Elongated, thick, arching stems support long-lasting blooms that fade from deep to light pink with age. The blooms tend to be mottled by rain. Bright red oval hips and bronze fall foliage follow the summer flowers.

Other names: none
Flower color: bright carmine pink; white centers
Flower size: 2–3"
Scent: light to none
Height: 15–20'
Spread: 10–12'
Blooms: mid-spring to mid-summer; no repeat blooming
Hardiness zones: 4–9

✿ Though this rose begins to bloom a little later than most ramblers, the flowers last a long time. The flowers are perfect for cutting and simple arrangements.

✿ This rose has more impact if it is allowed to reach its mature height rather than being pruned into a smaller shrub. Once established, it requires little attention.

✿ Relatively disease free, American Pillar is somewhat prone to powdery mildew in locations with poor air circulation.

✿ This rose is ideal for a coastal setting. It tolerates shade and poor soils but resents hot, dry weather.

Belle of Portugal

Other names: Belle Portugaise

Flower color: pale peach pink with dark pink reverse

Flower size: 4–6"

Scent: delicate, fruity

Height: 20'

Spread: 20'

Blooms: early spring into summer; once-blooming

Hardiness zones: 6–10

Belle of Portugal may only bloom once but it bears hundreds of flowers at a time during its long blooming cycle beginning in late spring. Each flower begins with a 4" long bud borne on pendulous stems. It opens into a semi-double flower with silky, quilled or reflexed petals. The flowers exude a delicate and fruity aroma atop glossy, olive green foliage. Belle of Portugal isn't terribly hardy owing to its *R. gigantean* parentage, but for most Northern California gardeners hardiness isn't likely an issue, and this rose has almost naturalized itself throughout the state.

✿ This vigorous rose is a favorite in locations throughout the country that experience temperate winters, but it won't grow at all in some parts of North America.

✿ Often considered a climbing tea, Belle of Portugal is great for growing on a high wall or fence. It is hardy enough for any Northern California garden and highly resistant to disease.

✿ It was bred at the botanical gardens in Lisbon and introduced in 1903.

Blaze Improved

Blaze Improved was bred in Czechoslovakia and introduced by Jackson & Perkins in 1950. As popular now as it was then, it bears abundant clusters of pure red, fully double blossoms that emit a lovely light and fruity scent. Widely used as a climber throughout Northern California, Blaze Improved has largely replaced the original Blaze, which has little to no repeat blooming. Blaze Improved blooms reliably in the heat of summer when most roses are resting.

❀ It blooms on old and new wood and tolerates salt.
❀ Blaze Improved blooms most profusely when it is trained horizontally along a fence. It produces a profusion of lateral side shoots, each of which ends in a flower cluster.

This winter-hardy rose is easy to grow and resistant to disease.

Other names: Demokracie, Blaze Superior, Imperial Blaze, New Blaze

Flower color: pure red

Flower size: 2–3"

Scent: light, fruity

Height: 8–10'

Spread: 6–8'

Blooms: spring to fall; repeat blooming

Hardiness zones: 4–10

Climbing Cécile Brünner

This beloved old-timer is a very vigorous climber and even stronger than its parent Cécile Brünner, a shorter polyantha. It bears large, airy clusters of small, pointed, pastel buds and creamy pink blossoms. The blossoms are perfectly shaped and fully double in form, opening from scrolled buds. They're borne singly and in well-spaced clusters. The flowers mostly bloom in spring on old wood. The foliage is dull and a little sparse but very healthy and clean. This climbing polyantha sport was discovered in 1894 by Hosp in the US.

Other names: Mlle. Cécile Brünner, Climbing Mignon, Climbing Mme. Cécile Brünner, Climbing Sweetheart Rose

Flower color: light pink

Flower size: 1¹/₂"

Scent: sweet, slightly spicy

Height: 18–25'

Spread: 20'

Blooms: spring to fall; repeat blooming

Hardiness zones: 4–9

❀ This rose blooms prolifically and sporadically into fall, on stems that reach for the sky. It is ideal for climbing up a warm wall, growing through trees and covering buildings or sturdy pergolas.

❀ Climbing Cécile Brünner is a long-lived variety with almost thornless stems. It is very difficult to propagate because of the scarcity of budding eyes.

❀ The flowers resemble those of its parent Cécile Brünner. The climber is sometimes mistaken for Cécile Brünner or Bloomfield Abundance.

❀ This rose was often called the 'boutonniere rose' because it frequently adorned buttonholes in the early 1900s.

This climber will tolerate some shade but prefers a hot, sunny location.

Don Juan

Don Juan is the best of the scented, dark red climbers. It has stood the test of time since its introduction in 1958. Don Juan is easily found all across the country in a wide range of climates as a result of its popularity and proven consistency in all regions. Large buds emerge on new and old wood, opening into shapely red blossoms. Each fully double blossom is made up of 30 to 35 petals in a cupped form. The strongly scented flowers bloom and bloom throughout the season on tall, wiry canes. Don Juan is highly rated by gardeners and the ARS, and will continue to be one of the best climbers available for years to come.

✿ This climber is ideal for growing against walls, pillars and pergolas, over arches and up a trellis. It is very versatile, reaching a reasonable size without overpowering its support.

✿ It is tolerant to extreme heat and bears beautiful hips immediately after the flower cycle is complete.

Other names: Climbing Don Juan
Flower color: deep velvety red
Flower size: 5"
Scent: strong rose
Height: 12–14'
Spread: 10–12'
Blooms: spring to fall; repeat blooming
Hardiness zones: 4–9

Don Juan experiences the best color when the temperatures at night are warmest.

Dortmund

Other names: none
Flower color: red with a white eye
Flower size: 3–4"
Scent: light apple
Height: 14–24'
Spread: 8–10'
Blooms: spring to fall; repeat blooming
Hardiness zones: 5–9

Few roses are rated as highly and respected as much as Dortmund, which has many excellent qualities. It grows tall and upright but dense in form. It bears large, single, deep red flowers with a glowing central white eye and bright yellow stamens. The single flowers have an average of five to eight petals. Dark glossy foliage complements the flower color.

✿ Dortmund requires reasonably good growing conditions to thrive. It is a little slow to bloom in spring, but once it takes off, the results are rewarding. It tolerates light, dappled shade and poorer soils and is highly disease resistant.

✿ This rose can grow large enough to cover one side of a small building. To create a medium shrub useful for hedging or as a specimen, prune to control the size. It can be trained up a pillar, veranda post, wall or trellis. It can also be grafted as a weeping standard.

✿ Deadhead heavily and frequently to encourage blooming. Discontinue deadheading at least five weeks before first frost to allow the plant to form a large crop of bright red hips in fall.

✿ Dortmund has received many awards including the Portland Gold Medal in 1971 and the Anerkannte Deutsche Rose Award in 1954.

This rose was introduced in 1955 by Kordes from Germany and was named after the city of Dortmund.

Dublin Bay

Dublin Bay is one of the best red-bloomed climbers available. It blooms longer and more frequently than just about any other climber. The first flush of blooms can last six weeks or more. On the west coast it bears stunning blossoms throughout the season. It has a reliable growth habit and weatherproof flowers and is low maintenance and highly disease resistant. Large oval buds emerge in spring on new and old wood and open to well-shaped, double blooms. The moderately thorny stems support dark green, shiny foliage.

Other names: Grandhotel
Flower color: bright red
Flower size: 4½"
Scent: moderate to strong
Height: 8–14'
Spread: 5–7'
Blooms: summer to fall; repeat blooming
Hardiness zones: 4–10

* Dublin Bay fans out well on low fences and trellises. It is attractive climbing up tripods, pillars, pergolas or arches. It can also be pruned into an informal hedge.
* This rose prefers full sun and moist, well-drained soil. It holds up well in cold or heat but should not be planted in windy locations.
* Dublin Bay was bred by Sam McGredy IV of New Zealand. Its color and structure come from Altissimo, and its free-flowering nature from its other parent, Bantry Bay. It was introduced in 1975 and won the Royal Horticultural Society Award of Garden Merit in 1993.

The rich, long-lasting flowers hold their color well even when cut for crafts or arrangements.

Flutterbye

Other names: Climbing Flutterbye

Flower color: yellow, coral, tangerine and pink blend

Flower size: 1½–2"

Scent: moderate, spicy

Height: 6–8'

Spread: 10'

Blooms: summer to fall; repeat blooming

Hardiness zones: 5–9

Bred by Tom Carruth in 1996, this climber is bound to become a classic over time.

Flutterbye is a beautiful rose that mimics the physical attributes of Mutabilis but in fiery tones. Classified as a climber, this variety doesn't reach its climbing counterparts' heights but it is still tall enough to climb a trellis or obelisk. Its most identifiable and unique feature is its flowers. Each flower is uniquely colored in yellow or apricot with hints of pink, orange, red and every warm color in between atop shiny, clean foliage. Each of the five to eight petals are ruffled and arranged in such a way that they almost resemble butterflies in flight, hence the name. This is a must-have for anyone with a small spot begging for a colorful climber.

✿ In mild climates, Flutterbye is often used as a pillar climber because of its size and form, but it remains a more balanced and rounded shrub in harsher regions.

✿ Generally Flutterbye is a rounded to fountainous rose, but with light pruning, you can shape it as you desire. You can also allow it to climb without much attention at all.

Fourth of July

Fourth of July was the first climbing rose awarded the All-American Rose Selection in over 20 years. It received this prestigious honor in 1999, when it was introduced by hybridizer Tom Carruth of Weeks Roses. This colorful climber has also received accolades in the UK, including the Breeders' Choice Award. Known as Crazy for You in England, this rose was named to celebrate America's independence. Often trained on fences, arbors and trellises, this climber bears large sprays of velvety, apple-scented blooms. Each semi-double bloom consists of 10 to 16 ruffled petals covered in unique stripes, speckles and combinations thereof. Bright yellow centers surround the prominent cluster of stamens in each bloom.

❁ Fourth of July is best grown in moderately moist, slightly acidic, well-drained soil. It can tolerate some shade but thrives in full sun.

❁ This rose will remain smaller in locations with colder winters and shorter seasons. With training it could be grown as a shrub rather than a climber.

❁ The deep green foliage provides a dramatic background for the long blooming season. The foliage is unaffected by disease and remains fresh and crisp in appearance.

Fourth of July always seems to be covered with a profusion of blooms on Independence Day.

Other names: Crazy for You, Hanabi

Flower color: velvety scarlet red with white stripes

Flower size: 2–3"

Scent: sweet, apple

Height: 8–10'

Spread: 3–6'

Blooms: spring to fall; repeat blooming

Hardiness zones: 4–9

Golden Showers

A treat for those of us who are crazy for yellow roses, Golden Showers is considered the best yellow climber in California. It bears flowers the shade of bright spring daffodils. They first emerge as long buds, opening quickly into loose, semi-double blossoms made up of 25 to 28 ruffled petals each. They're borne singly and in clusters, opening almost flat. The 4" wide blossoms exude a sweet licorice fragrance all summer long. Golden Showers was the creation of Dr. Walter Lammerts in 1956.

Other names: none

Flower color: bright yellow

Flower size: 4"

Scent: moderate, sweet, licorice

Height: 10–12'

Spread: 7'

Blooms: summer to fall; repeat blooming

Hardiness zones: 5–9

❀ The deep yellow flowers fade to a creamy yellow. Cooler temperatures give this free-flowering rose the best color and size. The flowers drop cleanly from the plant with continuity of bloom.

❀ The stiff, upright branches react well to pruning, and foliage is highly resistant to disease and requires little care or maintenance.

❀ Golden Showers grows well against a wall or pillar and if pruned hard, it may be grown as a shrub.

This vigorous climbing rose received the AARS designation along with three additional honors in 1957.

Handel

Handel is one of the most delicate climbing roses available. In full bloom, it displays a profusion of semi-double, white and creamy-centered blossoms edged in deep pink. The slender buds open to loosely double, wavy blooms in mid-summer and bloom less frequently as fall approaches. The glossy, dark foliage is only mildly affected by blackspot, and the flowers can withstand a rainfall without any damage. It develops slowly but gradually increases in vigor and performance as it ages.

* This rose is a strong grower, and the upright, stiff stems grow best on a fence, wall, arbor or pergola. Handel can be trained as a shrub with moderate pruning. The pruning will not affect the bloom-ing cycles because this rose bears flowers on new and old wood.
* The mid-season blooms sometimes look ragged, but a little deadheading will remedy that and also encourage further flowering in larger quantities.
* The young flowers are neatly formed and high centered, reminiscent of hybrid tea blooms, and open cupped in wide clusters. These blooms look best when grown during cooler periods or in cooler locations, but they still thrive in the heat.
* Handel has received many awards, including the Portland Gold Medal in 1975.

Other names:
Haendel, Händel, Macha

Flower color: white; pink edges

Flower size: 3$\frac{1}{2}$–4"

Scent: little to none

Height: 12–15'

Spread: 4–8'

Bloom period: spring to fall; repeat blooming

Hardiness zones: 5–9

Madame Alfred Carrière

Other names: none

Flower color: creamy white

Flower size: 2¹/₂–3 "

Scent: sweet, fresh and tea-like

Height: 15–18'

Spread: 10–12'

Blooms: spring to fall; repeat blooming

Hardiness zones: 4–9

Mildew can be a problem, but this rose is generally disease resistant and maintenance free.

Madame Alfred Carrière is considered one of the best noisettes ever developed. It was introduced in 1879, somewhat later than most other noisettes. It can still be found climbing the high wall of a cottage in Sissinghurst Castle Garden in southern England. It bears clusters of long-lasting, flattish, double flowers. The flowers open from pink pearl buds that are suitable for cutting. Each petal has a touch of yellow at the base, but only toward the center of the blossom. Large, semi-glossy leaves with serrated edges are vigorously produced on smooth, arching stems, resulting in upright, strong growth.

✿ This reliable rose is excellent for climbing walls, trees, trellises or pergolas. Thanks to its flexible, arching canes, this rose can easily be trained as a hedge.

✿ Madame Alfred Carrière tolerates some shade or a north wall, although the flowering will not be as profuse as it would be in a bright and sunny location. It is moderately winter hardy and better left unpruned.

✿ This rose was bred by Joseph Swartz in France. It was voted the 'best white climber' in 1908 by the National Rose Society of England. After his death, Swartz's widow went on to develop roses, including Mme. Ernst Calvat and Roger Lambelin.

New Dawn

New Dawn is one of the all-time favorite climbing varieties among gardeners and rosarians. Dr. William Van Fleet of the US originally introduced the hybrid seedling in 1910. In the 1920s, a repeat-blooming sport was introduced as The New Dawn. During the 1997 Triennial Convention in Benelux, members of the World Federation of Rose Societies elected New Dawn into the Hall of Fame. It was celebrated as the first patented plant in the world.

❀ New Dawn is known for its double flowers that fade from soft pink to a more pinkish white.

❀ The blossoms are borne singly and in small clusters. It bears plentiful, shiny foliage on upright, arching canes. The foliage is mildly prone to mildew on the tips of the stems later in the season but otherwise is disease resistant.

❀ Considered one of the easiest climbers to grow, this rose is suitable for pergolas, walls, fences, arches or pillars, or it can be pruned as a hedge or shrub. It is also a good rose for exhibition. It tolerates growing on a north-facing wall.

Other names:
Everblooming Dr. W. Van Fleet, The New Dawn
Flower color: pale pearl pink
Flower size: 3–3½"
Scent: sweet and fresh, apple
Height: 15–20'
Spread: 10–15'
Blooms: early spring to fall; repeat blooming
Hardiness zones: 4–9

Rosarium Uetersen

Rosarium Uetersen is a Kordesii climber developed in Kordes, Germany, in 1977, but its appearance might make you think it's hundreds of years old. It bears large, prolific clusters of very double, wide, flat blooms in early summer and intermittently later in the season. Each flower has 100 to 145 rounded petals that turn silvery pink as they age. It also produces an abundance of large, glossy, light foliage.

❀ This climber will grow successfully on a wall, pillar or arch. It will completely cover a fence or obelisk. It can also be pruned as a shrub rose.

❀ This rose is highly resistant to disease and it weathers very well.

❀ It was named after the rose garden at Uetersen in northern Germany.

❀ Rosarium Uetersen is definitely worth seeking out, despite its limited distribution.

Other names: Uetersen, Seminole Wind

Flower color: deep pink

Flower size: 3¹/₂–4"

Scent: mild, sweet green apples

Height: 10–12'

Spread: 6–10'

Blooms: spring to fall; repeat blooming

Hardiness zones: 5–10

Royal Sunset

Royal Sunset bears an abundance of dense, leathery, dark green foliage. Its bronze and copper foliar highlights complement the bright summery blossoms. Intense apricot orange blossoms fade to a soft pink tinged with apricot hues. It will bloom on new and old wood. The flowers, borne in clusters, are cupped, semi-double and look like hybrid tea blooms. It blooms profusely throughout summer and well into fall.

Other names: none

Flower color: apricot pink with blended yellow

Flower size: 4^1/$_2$–5"

Scent: strong and fruity

Height: 6–10'

Spread: 6'

Blooms: mid-spring to late summer; repeat blooming

Hardiness zones: 5–10

❀ Most apricot-colored climbers have leggy growth habits, but Royal Sunset does not. It produces bushy, stiff growth that is best suited to growing against walls or fences or in a large area where it can be fanned out onto a support.

❀ Heavy reddish canes and attractive hips will provide color well into winter in milder climates.

❀ The plant requires winter protection in areas and microclimates colder than zone 5. A mulch of straw or wood shavings will insulate the plant.

❀ Royal Sunset was awarded the Portland Gold Medal in 1960, the year it was introduced.

Royal Sunset was introduced in 1960 by Dr. Denison Morey.

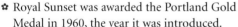

Sombreuil

Other names: Colonial White, Mlle. de Sombreuil

Flower color: white

Flower size: 3½–4"

Scent: sweet green apple

Height: 12–15'

Spread: 6–8'

Blooms: mid-spring to late summer; repeat blooming

Hardiness zones: 6–9

Sombreuil is the oldest climbing hybrid tea rose. It was introduced in 1851 in France and typifies the classic old rose style. It bears large, white, double, somewhat muddled flowers that occasionally display a touch of pink and yellow. The refined, quilled petals open flat into quartered, doubled blossoms. Each flower consists of 100 petals, and the blooms blend beautifully with the semi-glossy, medium green leaves on purplish green, moderately thorny canes.

❧ This rose is suitable for climbing pillars, trellises, arbors, old trees and pergolas. It is easy to grow and is resistant to rust and blackspot. It benefits from a location in full sun and tends to lose a little of its form and size in a shady spot.

❧ Deadheading, thinning, removing dead canes and light pruning will improve the flowering performance, growth habit and vigor.

❧ This rose was named after Mlle. de Sombreuil, a heroine from the French Revolution.

Westerland

Westerland bears clusters of freshly scented, double, bright orangy apricot flowers. Each petal is ruffled with serrated or scalloped edges. The semi-glossy, dark green foliage is generally resistant to disease.

* The old canes can be pruned out every few years to encourage new, dense growth and prolonged blooming.
* Sturdy, stiff, moderately thorny canes allow this variety to climb pillars, pergolas and veranda posts. Plant it in the back of a mixed border once it's been pruned into a shrub form.
* Some claim that in milder climates it can reach 15' tall as an upright, well-branched climber.
* Widely grown and available since its 1969 introduction, Westerland won the Anerkannte Deutsche Rose in 1974.

Other names: none
Flower color: bright apricot orange with yellow on the petals' reverse
Flower size: 3–3¹⁄₂"
Scent: fruity, spicy
Height: 10–12'
Spread: 4–5'
Bloom period: spring to fall; repeat blooming
Hardiness: zones 5–9

HYBRID TEA

The first hybrid teas were bred around 1867, a turning point for roses. With the introduction of these roses, the era of old garden roses ended and the era of modern roses began. Hybrid teas are the dominant roses in the cut-flower industry and the garden. They are upright bushes with strong, prickly canes and usually have one flower per cane. Hybrid teas bloom continually throughout the growing season until a hard fall frost. The flowers are large, double blooms with a pointed form and an extensive color range that includes all colors except blue, black and green. Some varieties are intensely fragrant.

Hybrid teas may need winter protection in the coldest zones throughout Northern California. Use hybrid teas in a formal rose garden or cut-flower garden, in borders or as specimens. Hybrid teas can also be grown in containers, although they will require further care and protection to survive the winter successfully.

Barbra Streisand

Other names: none
Flower color: pinkish lavender
Flower size: 4–5"
Scent: old rose and citrus
Height: 3–4'
Spread: 24–36"
Blooms: spring to fall; repeat blooming
Hardiness zones: 5–9

The flowers are borne on long, straight stems, allowing for fantastic cut flowers.

An avid gardener, Barbra Streisand approached Tom Carruth of Weeks Roses in 1996 and asked him to create a rose for her. He chose three seedlings for her to try, and nine months later she selected this rose. It is fragrant, naturally vigorous and disease resistant, and is now featured in the singer's Malibu rose garden, which contains over 1200 roses. It bears sprays of highly fragrant lavender blossoms. The petal edges are somewhat darker, and the depth of that color changes depending on the time of year. Each fully double flower is made up of 35 or more petals and sits atop deep green, glossy foliage. This dusty mauve-pink rose has all the qualities one could want from a modern hybrid tea, and it is destined to be a classic.

✿ This rose is fairly upright and bushy. It may need a little pruning every couple of years to encourage a dense growth habit. It is a healthy rose for its color class but not completely disease free. Take the necessary precautions to prevent disease.

✿ Locations with milder temperatures produce the best flower color and mature size. This rose tolerates high winds and salt air and therefore suits a coastal garden.

Although this rose blooms prolifically throughout the growing season, dead-heading will further extend flowering.

Bride's Dream

Long, pointed buds emerge from the tips of long, elegant stems, perfect for a bride's bouquet. Bride's Dream is known for its perfect form and exceptionally rapid repeat bloom. It is reminiscent of its parent, Royal Highness, but it displays a vast improvement in vigor, productivity and disease resistance. It is considered one of the best overall pale pink roses, bearing double, high-centered blossoms made up of 25 to 30 petals each. The healthy, dark green foliage covers moderately thorny canes to produce a dense and upright shrub.

✿ Bride's Dream's tall stature is ideal for the back of a border. It also makes a wonderful specimen plant when left to its own devices.

✿ The healthy foliage seems unaffected by stress and environmental conditions. It doesn't suffer from blackspot, rust or mildew, which can cause problems in parts of Northern California.

✿ This rose produces more than enough blossoms for cutting and arrangements.

✿ Bride's Dream was bred by W. Kordes Söhne Roses in Germany. It was introduced into commerce in 1986.

Other names: Fairytale Queen, Märchenkönigin
Flower color: pale pastel pink
Flower size: 4$1/2$–5$1/2$"
Scent: slight
Height: 4$1/2$–5$1/2$'
Spread: 4'
Blooms: spring to fall; repeat blooming
Hardiness zones: 6–9

The flowers are known to pout a little during sudden temperature changes.

Crystalline

Other names: Valerie Swane

Flower color: white

Flower size: 5"

Scent: medium, spicy and sweet tea

Height: 4–6'

Spread: 4–5'

Blooms: spring to fall; repeat blooming

Hardiness zones: 6–9

The flowers may spot in damp coastal conditions. Overall, this rose performs best where summers are hot.

Crystalline was initially bred for the florist trade and greenhouse production but has proven itself an excellent garden rose too. Frequently used for exhibition, this rose blooms in profusion, singly or in clusters, on long canes. The flowers are especially large and well formed. Each flower is made up of 30 to 35 petals that form into a high-centered to cupped bloom. A sweet, spicy tea aroma wafts from the pure white blooms throughout the summer months. Large, globular orange hips form after the flowering has finished for the season. The foliage is unique in appearance as the leaves are exceptionally crinkled for a hybrid tea.

✿ Crystalline grows into an upright, bushy shrub. Each cane is covered in standard light green prickles. This rose may require support as it reaches maturity.

✿ Considered to be generally resistant to disease, this variety is a little prone to mildew. Take the necessary precautions when choosing the perfect location for this rose.

✿ Crystalline is an ideal rose for the cutting garden. The flowers have a vase life of four to eight days.

Dainty Bess

Dainty Bess, named after the hybridizer's wife, is still as popular and beautiful today as it was when it was first introduced in 1925. Its single, ruffled, light pink flowers make it one of the most unusual hybrid tea varieties available. Rose stamens are usually yellow, and only 10 percent of roses have burgundy stamens. Dainty Bess is one of these rarities. The flowers are produced either singly or in clusters on very thorny, sturdy canes. When Dainty Bess is in flower, it truly is one of the most beautiful roses you could ever imagine.

✿ This rose isn't ideal for cutting because the flowers are short lived and the plant is so compact.
✿ The blossoms of this variety close at night, which is very unusual for roses.
✿ A climbing form of Dainty Bess is available, with blooms similar to those of the original shrub form.
✿ Among other awards, Dainty Bess received the 1925 Royal National Rose Society Gold Medal.

Other names: The Artistic Rose
Flower color: pale pink
Flower size: 3$^1/_2$–4"
Scent: light tea
Height: 24–30"
Spread: 24"
Blooms: spring to fall; repeat blooming
Hardiness zones: 6–9

Diana, Princess of Wales

Other names: The Work Continues

Flower color: pink, pale yellow and ivory blend

Flower size: 4–5"

Scent: moderate

Height: 4–5'

Spread: 4'

Blooms: spring to fall; repeat blooming

Hardiness zones: 6–9

This rose is a fitting tribute to Princess Diana. It's gracious in appearance, classic, beautiful and elegant yet understated. A blend of pale creamy yellow emerges from the center and melds into creamy shades of salmon pink, which darken on each petal edge. This color combination results in a refined form suitable for exhibition or just about any garden setting. The very double flowers are made up of 26 to 40 petals borne in small clusters. Moderately scented, the flowers are produced on long stems, covered only slightly with prickles and perfect for cutting and arrangements.

✿ This rose is highly resistant to disease and is easy to care for. The results speak for themselves.

✿ Dr. Keith W. Zary created this beauty for Jackson & Perkins in the US. It was launched in July 1998 in honor of Princess Diana. A percentage of the net sales of this rose helps to raise funds for The Diana, Princess of Wales Memorial Fund, which contributes to the humanitarian causes that were important to the Princess.

Double Delight

Double Delight is aptly named, as it delights with its strong, sweet fragrance and its unique flower color. The only drawback is that the plant will very likely experience mildew or blackspot, or both. But don't let that stop you, because it is one of the most popular roses available and it's worth growing for the fragrance alone! The fully double, high-centered flowers open cream with red edges and gradually darken to solid red. The color prompted the French to name this variety *La Rose de Rouge à Lèvres*, 'The Lipstick Rose.'

❀ The unique color makes this beauty hard to place in a bed or border, so it is better used as a specimen. It is also suitable for containers, where it can be easily monitored for disease.

❀ A 1977 All-America Rose Selection, Double Delight grows well in a greenhouse or a warm, dry location. Keep this variety in full sun for the best color contrast.

❀ Rain doesn't seem to affect the blooms, but cool, wet weather can promote mildew. Blackspot can also be a problem.

❀ No two flowers are alike. Heat intensifies the bloom color while in cooler temperatures the color becomes more subtle. The award-winning fragrance is unaffected by temperature, light or age.

Flower color: cream; carmine red edges

Flower size: 5–5½"

Scent: strong, sweet with hint of spice

Height: 3–4'

Spread: 24–36"

Blooms: spring to fall; repeat blooming

Hardiness zones: 6–9

Double Delight is a long-lasting cut flower, a good choice for competition and exhibition.

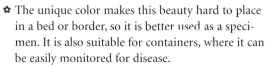

Electron

Electron is a compact, tidy rose bearing leathery foliage and large, high-centered, fully double flowers. The blooms hold color well but are a little slow to open. Each flower is made up of an average of 30 to 40 velvety petals. Electron has a classic hybrid tea form, excellent for competition and exhibition. It is known for its rich fragrance and vibrant fuchsia pink color.

Other names: Mullard Jubilee
Flower color: deep pink
Flower size: 4–5"
Scent: sweet and strong
Height: 3–4¹/₂'
Spread: 3–4'
Blooms: spring to fall; repeat blooming
Hardiness zones: 6–10

Electron's other common name came from a celebrated electronic company known for its significant technological advances in the UK.

✿ The average rose gardener will appreciate this rose, which requires very little maintenance and is moderately disease resistant. The glowing reddish pink blooms can be seen from a distance and withstand just about any type of weather.

✿ The long-lasting flowers are ideal for cutting. Cut while in bud, as the blooms are just about to unfurl, to extend their vase life.

✿ This rose requires more moderate temperatures, so plant it away from surfaces that reflect heat.

✿ In 1973, only three years after its introduction, Electron was awarded the prestigious All-America Rose Selection.

Elina

Elina is one of the best of its color and class. It is the perfect rose for the beginner to use as an exhibition variety, and its long stems make it a great cut flower. Slightly delayed flowering extends the bloom season. The blooms are evenly petaled, double and high centered. The bushy foliage has large, dark, slightly red-tinted leaves.

Other names: Peaudouce

Flower color: ivory white; yellow center

Flower size: 5½–6"

Scent: very light

Height: 3–5'

Spread: 3'

Blooms: spring to fall; repeat blooming

Hardiness zones: 6–9

✿ While many light-colored blooms get mottled or spotty after rain, the flowers of this variety stand up well in rain.

✿ Elina is regarded as one of the most reliable and free-blooming hybrid teas available. It is almost always in bloom and boasts huge blossoms.

✿ In 1987, Elina was named the Anerkannte Deutsche Rose and received the New Zealand (Gold Star) Gold Medal; in 1994 it was awarded the James Mason Gold Medal.

✿ It boasts outstanding vigor, form and resistance to disease.

✿ This rose used to be known as Peaudouce, French for 'soft skin.' The name was changed after a brand of infant diapers of the same name was introduced.

Elizabeth Taylor

Other names: none

Flower color: deep pink with darker edges

Flower size: 4¹/₂–5"

Scent: moderate, spicy

Height: 4–5'

Spread: 5–5¹/₂'

Blooms: spring to fall, repeat blooming

Hardiness zones: 6–9

Elizabeth Taylor prefers a warm climate and performs best in moderate temperatures.

Elizabeth Taylor, named in honor of Hollywood royalty, is popular with exhibitors and gardeners. Von C. Weddle, an amateur hybridizer in Indiana, bred this rose in 1985. Elizabeth Taylor has a well-branched form, a vigorous and upright growth habit and long, moderately thorny stems tipped with classic, long-lived flowers. Each spicy-scented flower is borne in a double form, consisting of 30 to 35 petals. They usually emerge singly with high centers. The dark green foliage is healthy and semi-glossy in appearance. In rare instances, a striped petal may occur in shades of light pink or white.

❀ This rose, although upright in habit, tends to spread a little. It's best planted in the middle or back of a rose or mixed border, or left as a beautiful specimen to show off its attributes.

❀ This rose repeats well all season and requires little care. It is highly resistant to disease and thrives in the California sun.

Fragrant Cloud

Although its full, bright coral red flowers are beautiful in their own right, Fragrant Cloud is known for its outstanding, unique fragrance. It has won seven awards for its beauty and fragrance, including the Gamble Fragrance Award in 1970. The ARS considers it one of the top 10 fragrant roses, which is a great accomplishment for a hybrid tea that was only introduced in 1963. The World Federation of Rose Societies' Hall of Fame rated it third best of all time.

Other names: Nuage Parfumé

Flower color: orangy red

Flower size: 5"

Scent: intense and strong

Height: 4–5'

Spread: 32–36"

Blooms: spring to fall; repeat blooming

Hardiness zones: 5–9

❀ Fragrant Cloud has a bushy and upright growth habit with well-branched canes, which support glossy, dark green foliage. In typical hybrid tea form, the full and evenly petaled flowers are high centered, double and made up of more than 30 petals each.

❀ It is ideal for borders and beds and requires little maintenance other than seasonal deadheading and a little spring pruning.

❀ Fragrant Cloud has received numerous honors and awards, most in recognition of its outstanding scent.

Fragrant Cloud is only mildly prone to mildew in the fall and blackspot in damp weather.

Gemini

Other names: none
Flower color: creamy, pale pink with darker pink edges
Flower size: 4½–5"
Scent: moderate, sweet
Height: 5½'
Spread: 5'
Blooms: spring to fall; repeat blooming
Hardiness zones: 6–9

Gemini is an All-American Rose Selection from 1999.

Gemini is exceptional in a number of ways. It exhibits an excellent flower form, fantastic color, vigor and disease-free, healthy foliage. Gemini is almost the perfect rose. Its petals have good substance but are not too plentiful, and it still produces and maintains beautiful blooms during damp coastal weather. Gemini boasts a number of other favorable qualities as well. It's easy to care for, a reliable bloomer and it performs beautifully throughout the growing season. Although only introduced in 2000, it is ranked 23rd in exhibition standings in the US. It will likely be included in the top 10 roses for exhibition purposes in the near future.

✿ Whether you're growing Gemini as a garden or exhibition rose, the flowers last and last, in bouquets and on the plant.

✿ As the large, bicolored blooms mature, the coral-on-cream shading intensifies.

✿ After Dr. Keith W. Zary bred this rose in 1999, a committee in Medford, Oregon, named it Gemini based on the two-toned or 'twin' coloration effect of coral and cream.

✿ Gemini is a stout, well-anchored bush with high-centered blooms and long stems clothed in healthy foliage.

Gift of Life

Harkness Roses in England bred this rose in 1999. It represents the hope of those who have benefited from organ and tissue donation. Gift of Life is also the flagship for organ donation fundraising and awareness. This breathtaking double rose bears 26 to 40 petals in a pink and yellow blend. The flowers emit a sweet and light fragrance. The stems are clothed in many prickles and large, glossy foliage. It grows into a medium, bushy form suitable for just about any garden setting. It has won a number of awards including the Breeders' Choice Award in 1997 and the Belfast Gold Medal in 1999.

Other names: Poetry in Motion
Flower color: pink with yellow reverse
Flower size: 4"
Scent: sweet and light
Height: 3–4'
Spread: 2–3'
Blooms: spring to fall; repeat blooming
Hardiness zones: 6–9

✿ The foliage is healthy and clean, resistant to all disease.
✿ The flowers are generally borne singly but occasionally grow in a small cluster.
✿ Gift of Life was a result of crossing Dr. Darley and Elina, two fine parents with much to offer.

Honor

Other names:
Honour, Michele Torr
Flower color: white
Flower size: 4–5"
Scent: light
Height: 5–5½'
Spread: 4–5'
Blooms: late spring to fall; repeat blooming
Hardiness zones: 5–9

Honor was introduced in 1980 as part of the All American Series along with two other roses, Love (p. 236) and Cherish. Honor clearly has exhibition quality, winning the Portland Gold Medal in 1978 and the All-America Selection in 1980. This rose has a tall, upright and vigorous growth habit and bears satiny white buds that open to large blossoms with golden stamens. The flowers bloom in clusters or singly on long, moderately thorny canes and are suitable for cutting and arrangements. Each flower has 25–30 clear, velvety petals.

✿ Honor is a tender rose in cooler climates, so winter protection may be necessary.
✿ This rose produces long, strong stems ideal for cutting. To extend the vase life of the flowers, cut the stems when the blooms are in bud.
✿ Honor is perfectly suited to mixed borders and beds or works well as a stunning specimen.

You don't have to be a rose aficionado to successfully grow this variety, as it is highly disease resistant and easy to maintain.

Just Joey

Just Joey is treasured for its unusual coloration; its blooms emerge a soft coppery brown with buff pink hues. It bears fully double, rounded flowers with lightly serrated, wavy petal edges. The blooms open from long, elegant buds borne singly or in large, loose clusters. Each large flower is made up of at least 30 petals, exposing dark golden stamens. The attractive yet sparse leaves are large, glossy and resistant to most diseases. It has a vigorous sprawling and open growth habit, and it becomes bushy and upright in form.

* Just Joey's rich flower color and open form are unique among large-flowered hybrid teas. The flowers are excellent for cutting and garden exhibits, and are valued by floral designers.
* Though soft, the flower color isn't likely to be overwhelmed by other vivid flowering plants, making this rose ideal for mixed beds and borders or as a small specimen.
* It received the World's Favorite Rose award in 1994, the Royal National Rose Society James Mason Gold Medal in 1986 and the Royal Horticultural Society Award of Garden Merit in 1993.

This rose was hybridized in 1973 by Roger Pawsey from Cants of Colchester in England.

Other names: none
Flower color: apricot-orange blend
Flower size: 4–5"
Scent: sweet and fruity
Height: 30"–4'
Spread: 24–36"
Blooms: summer to autumn; repeat blooming
Hardiness zones: 5–9

Liebeszauber

Other names:
Crimson Spire
Flower color: dark red
Flower size: 6–7"
Scent: very sweet
Height: 3½–6'
Spread: 3½'
Blooms: summer to fall;
repeat blooming
Hardiness zones: 5–9

Liebeszauber is a vigorous rose with an upright growth habit. The foliage emerges red in early spring and matures to a deep, dark green. The pure dark red blossoms are loosely cupped, wavy-petaled and sweetly fragrant.

✿ The strong stems are suitable for cutting or training. This rose would be ideal for exhibiting at a rose show or for display planting in a mixed border. It is best planted at the back of borders because it is so vigorous—the occasional shoot reaches heights of 6½' if left intact.

✿ This hybrid tea blooms like a floribunda, bearing its flowers singly and in clusters that stand up well in the rain.

✿ Liebeszauber has a tendency to send up spindly canes occasionally, but these are easily removed with a quick snip. A more manageable, balanced bush can be trained by pinching out the side buds. This rose requires a hard prune each year.

The name of this rose is German for 'love's magic.'

Marilyn Monroe

Tom Carruth chose a fitting name for this beautiful creation. Marilyn Monroe is an elegant, memorable rose reminiscent of the American legend. Although new, it's hard to forget. The classically formed, shapely flowers consist of 30 to 35 petals. The soft colors and delicate-looking petals disguise their strength. Each petal is full of substance. The outer petals are washed in green chlorophyll, which helps feed the flowers once they've been cut, lengthening their life on the plant and in the vase. Marilyn Monroe has the longest vase life of any apricot rose. It produces copious amounts of flowers all season long and starts over again after a winter's rest.

Other names: none
Flower color: pale creamy apricot with hints of green
Flower size: 4–4^1/$_2$"
Scent: light citrus
Height: 4–6'
Spread: 4–5'
Blooms: early spring to mid-fall; repeat blooming
Hardiness zones: 6–9

- ✿ The foliage is healthy and resists disease.
- ✿ This rose is possibly the best apricot hybrid tea rose for hot weather.
- ✿ Marilyn Monroe is ideal for a cutting garden, classic English garden or mixed border. The flowers are neutral, suitable for a variety of fresh arrangements.
- ✿ It has an upright but slightly spreading growth habit.

This Tom Carruth creation was the result of crossing Sunset Celebration and St. Patrick.

Mellow Yellow

Other names: none
Flower color: medium yellow
Flower size: 4"
Scent: moderate, fruity
Height: 4–5'
Spread: 4'
Blooms: early spring to fall, repeat blooming
Hardiness zones: 6–9

The flowers have a tendency to grow a little larger in cooler weather.

Mellow Yellow is one of the best yellow hybrid tea roses to come along in recent years. The quality of flower color is outstanding: not too gold, pale or garish but pure, clean and clear. The flowers hold their color even as the blooms complete their cycle and the petals fall to the ground. It freely produces the fruity-scented flowers well into late fall. The stems are long and sturdy, able to support the large, urn-shaped flowers. Each flower is fully double, made up of 30 to 35 petals with good substance.

✿ Mellow Yellow is highly resistant to disease and easy to care for.

✿ This naturally vigorous rose is great for cutting. The flowers have a long life on the plant and in the vase.

Memorial Day

Tom Carruth of Weeks Roses bred this rose not only for its beauty but to honor, celebrate and remember those who fought and died for our freedom. A magnificent tribute, this strongly scented rose is unique in form. Each of its 50-plus petals has tattered edges clothed in a magical color. The tightly packed petals unfurl from pointed buds, resulting in fully double blossoms in an old-fashioned form with spiral centers. Rich green, healthy foliage adorns low-thorned stems, which are long enough for cutting. It only takes one flower to scent an entire room with fragrance reminiscent of damask roses from long ago.

✿ This rose thrives in hot weather. The flower color darkens as fall approaches.

✿ Memorial Day received the AARS designation in 2004, the year of its introduction.

✿ Memorial Day was a result of crossing Blueberry Hill and New Zealand.

Other names: none

Flower color: clear pink accented with lavender

Flower size: 5"

Scent: strong, classic old rose

Height: 3–4'

Spread: 3–4'

Blooms: spring to fall; repeat blooming

Hardiness zones: 6–9

Blueberry Hill (page 214) is a lilac-colored floribunda, and contributed its lavender coloration and sweet perfume. New Zealand (page 202) gave its offspring tightly packed, high centers and fragrance.

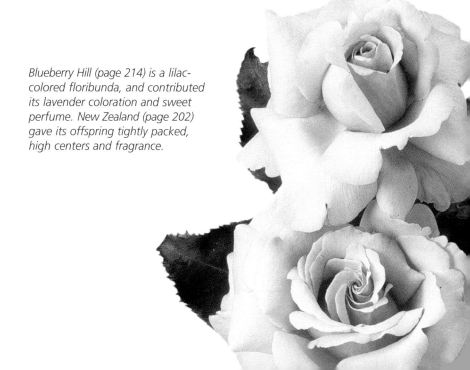

Mister Lincoln

Other names: Mr. A. Lincoln, Mr. Lincoln
Flower color: dark red
Flower size: 4–5¹/₂"
Scent: damask
Height: 4–5'
Spread: 30"–3¹/₂'
Blooms: spring to fall; repeat blooming
Hardiness zones: 5–9

This tough, dependable rose is one of the hardiest hybrid teas.

The blooms of Mister Lincoln are among the darkest red of any red rose. It was bred by Herbert C. Swim and O.L. Weeks in 1964 and boasts immense, velvety, deep red flowers and a scent reminiscent of damask roses. It has been one of the most popular hybrid tea roses in its color class and category since its release. The blossoms usually occur one to a stem. Urn-shaped buds open quickly in spring. The fully double flowers first emerge cupped, but soon produce a flat, classic, high-centered form. Each flower consists of 30 to 40 petals and displays the characteristics of Mister Lincoln's parents, Chrysler Imperial and Charles Mallerin. Dark, semi-glossy, leathery foliage enhances the flowers' beauty.

✿ Mister Lincoln is at its most beautiful when the flowers are almost open, exposing the bright yellow stamens.

✿ This rose prefers hot, dry conditions. The flowers and foliage won't burn in the hot sun as easily as other red roses will. The flower color will eventually fade to magenta.

✿ Use Mister Lincoln as a specimen in a garden or at the back of a rose bed or border.

✿ Mister Lincoln received AARS designation in 1965 and has remained one of the most popular roses. It continues to be one of California's favorites.

Moonstone

Moonstone is aptly named, as its pearly white and pink color emulates that gemstone. The large flowers are fully double, bearing 30 to 35 petals each, borne singly on tall stems. Each creamy white petal is finely edged with pale pink. This fades in time but the flowers still maintain their beauty and purity. This hybrid tea is a result of crossing Crystalline (page 186) and Lynn Anderson, another bicolored rose with prominent pink-edged, clear white petals.

Other names: Cadillac DeVille

Flower color: creamy ivory edged with delicate pink

Flower size: $4^{1}/_{2}$–5"

Scent: mild, tea and rose

Height: 4–6'

Spread: 4–5'

Blooms: early spring to fall; repeat blooming

Hardiness zones: 7–9

✿ Moonstone has a vase life of four to five days. The stems are long enough for cutting.

✿ This variety prefers some heat to bring out its best form.

✿ Moonstone was created by Tom Carruth of Weeks Roses in 1999.

Moonstone's cream and pink petals resemble the color of rainbow moonstone, an iridescent gemstone said to strengthen intuition and psychic perception, bringing balance to the lives of those who wear it.

New Zealand

Sam McGredy once said that new pink roses are very hard to sell. He must have had confidence in New Zealand, however, when he introduced the rose in 1991. New Zealand is likely the first rose to challenge Fragrant Cloud for its rich perfume. It is known not only for its beauty but its strong fragrance—one flower can scent a large space. Thirty to 35 pale, creamy pink petals make up each flower in a fully double form. The flowers are borne singly among deep green, glossy foliage. Overall, this variety has excellent form suitable for any garden setting.

Other names: Aotearoa-New Zealand, Aotearoa

Flower color: pale creamy pink

Flower size: 4$\frac{1}{2}$–5"

Scent: strong, honeysuckle

Height: 2$\frac{1}{2}$–5'

Spread: 2–3'

Blooms: early spring to fall; repeat blooming

Hardiness zones: 6–9

❀ New Zealand is resistant to both mildew and rust, and has an above-average resistance to blackspot.

❀ This rose prefers consistent temperatures and grows best when planted in a cool location.

❀ New Zealand easily blends into beds with a variety of colors.

❀ Breeder Sam McGredy named this rose 'Aotearoa' to commemorate the 150th anniversary of New Zealand. Aotearoa is Maori for 'Land of the Long White Cloud.'

Peace

Peace has been referred to as the Rose of the Century, and it is more than capable of living up to the title. It is very easy to grow and is one of the most famous roses ever produced. It has won many awards, including the All-America Selection in 1946. It is an upright grower with moderately thorny canes and large, glossy foliage. Even out of bloom, this shrub looks great. The yellow can pale in too much heat, while the pink intensifies.

✿ Peace is an ideal cut-flower variety. It is suitable for rose beds, hedges and borders. Considered one of the best varieties to grow as a standard, it is a little resentful of hard pruning but fares well with moderate to light pruning.

✿ Climbing Peace is a sport of Peace that can reach heights of 15 to 20 feet.

✿ Peace has a moderate level of disease resistance but is prone to blackspot in cooler climates. Its overall health has been compromised as a result of being cloned millions of times since its introduction in 1945.

✿ Peace, the first rose designated World's Favorite Rose by the World Federation of Rose Societies, received that honor in 1976.

✿ This rose was originally named after the breeder's mother, Claudia, but was renamed in the United States to celebrate the end of World War II and to remind us of the beauty of world peace.

Other names: Gloria Dei, Mme A. Meilland, Gioia, Beke, Fredsrosen
Flower color: soft yellow; baby pink edges
Flower size: 5$\frac{1}{2}$–6"
Scent: mild and fruity
Height: 5$\frac{1}{2}$–6$\frac{1}{2}$'
Spread: 3$\frac{1}{2}$–4'
Blooms: spring to fall; repeat blooming
Hardiness zones: 5–9

Pristine

This hybrid tea couldn't have received a better name. The overall form and allure of this delicate-looking rose is simple and unspoiled but elegant all the same. The ivory buds open into porcelain white, double flowers with blushed pink outer edges. Each lightly scented flower is made up of 25 to 30 petals surrounding bright yellow and amber stamens. It is sometimes hard to believe such delicate-looking flowers come from such a vigorous and robust shrub. It was bred by William A. Warriner in 1978 and introduced by Jackson & Perkins.

Other names: none

Flower color: white with a hint of pale pink on the petal edges

Flower size: 4¹/₂–6"

Scent: light

Height: 4–4¹/₂'

Spread: 3–3¹/₂'

Blooms: spring to fall; repeat blooming

Hardiness zones: 4–9

✿ The flowers are known to hold their color even in the most intense heat.

✿ The waxy and tough foliage is resistant to disease and contrasts well with the pale flowers. Mahogany red new leaves emerge throughout the season, adding color to this already colorful hybrid tea.

✿ Owing to its vigorous nature, the stems can be cut with little effect on blooming.

✿ Pristine makes a great cut flower, but once in a vase it has a tendency to drop petals soon after opening. For the longest display, cut the stems at the loose bud stage.

✿ Pristine is often described as nearly thornless, but the few thorns it has are very large.

✿ Pristine is one of the highest-rated exhibition hybrid teas on the market.

St. Patrick

St. Patrick was a result of crossing two great exhibition varieties. It is one of the few top award winners from an amateur breeder and is only the second variety from an amateur breeder to ever win the AARS distinction. St. Patrick is also one of the most unusually colored roses, displaying green tinted blossoms from apple green buds. The buds open slowly into fully double, high-pointed blossoms, providing a long-lasting, showy display throughout the summer months. Unusually thick petals are a rare quality for roses in general, but thick yellow petals are particularly rare. St. Patrick exhibits a number of unusual qualities that add to its success and popularity.

✿ If you plan to enter a rose show, St. Patrick may be your ideal candidate. It excels in exhibition and as a conversation piece.

✿ Summer heat is necessary to bring out its best attributes, including color and form. The color is affected by temperature as well. Hotter temperatures intensify the green coloration, while cool temperatures emphasize the yellow.

Other names: Limelight, Saint Patrick

Flower color: yellow with chartreuse on the outside petals

Flower size: 3¹/₂–5"

Scent: light

Height: 3–4'

Spread: 3–4'

Blooms: spring to fall; repeat blooming

Hardiness zones: 5–10

St. Patrick has excellent resistance to disease. It requires little care and is easy to grow.

Stainless Steel

Other names: none

Flower color: pale silvery gray lavender

Flower size: 5–6"

Scent: intense, sweet

Height: 4–5'

Spread: 4'

Blooms: early spring to fall; repeat blooming

Hardiness zones: 6–9

Stainless Steel is the 'new and improved' version of Sterling Silver, a hybrid tea bred by Fisher in 1957. The creation of Sterling Silver's unique color marked a breakthrough in rose breeding. Stainless Steel, however, is easier to care for and grow, and bears longer-lasting flowers. It still possesses its predecessor's scent and characteristic coloration. The well-formed, double flowers are very large and consist of 26 to 40 petals each. Borne singly and in small clusters, the flowers emerge from the tips of long stems clothed in semi-glossy, medium green foliage.

- ✿ Stainless Steel is highly resistant to disease. It requires little care and is considered easy to grow.
- ✿ It exhibits a classic show form bearing clear, crisp flowers. The flowers aren't affected by adverse weather and remain clean.
- ✿ The flower size and color is much better in locations with cooler temperatures.

Sunset Celebration

This All-America Rose Selection was named Warm Wishes when it was introduced to the American market, but the name was changed to Sunset Celebration to commemorate the 100th anniversary of *Sunset* magazine in 1998. Though many rose gardeners still call it Warm Wishes, its new name is appropriate because the rose exhibits almost every color of a California sunset. This evenly balanced bush bears large, fully double flowers made up of an average of 30 or more petals each. The long, elegant buds open up to a classic, high-centered spiral. The well-formed flowers are borne singly or in clusters atop dark, glossy foliage.

Other names: Warm Wishes, Chantoli, Exotic
Flower color: soft peachy coral
Flower size: 4¹/₂–5¹/₂"
Scent: sweet and fruity
Height: 3–5'
Spread: 24–30"
Blooms: spring to fall; repeat blooming
Hardiness zones: 4–9

❀ The flower color changes over time and varies depending on heat and moisture. It sometimes evolves from apricot or amber to a subtle shade of pink with peach tones.
❀ Sunset Celebration makes an impact planted en masse or as a specimen. It works well in mixed beds and borders and thrives in a container.
❀ This hybrid tea is establishing itself as one of the finest introductions of recent years, and it has received a number of awards.

The long-stemmed, colorful blooms are ideal for cutting, and the cut flowers last seven days or more.

Veteran's Honor

Other names: City of Newcastle Bicentennary, Five-Roses Rose, Lady in Red

Flower color: deep, bright red

Flower size: 5–5¹⁄₂"

Scent: slight, raspberry

Height: 4–5'

Spread: 5'

Blooms: spring to fall; repeat blooming

Hardiness zones: 6–9

Dr. Keith W. Zary of Jackson & Perkins bred Veteran's Honor in 1999. It was developed and named at the request of the former Veterans Administration Secretary for Health, Dr. Kenneth W. Kizer, as a living tribute to the women and men who served the United States of America. Veteran's Honor produces high-centered flowers in a double form made up of 26 to 40 velvety petals. The deep red petals darken toward the edges over time. The flowers are mostly borne singly atop upright stems covered in dark, semi-glossy foliage.

✿ Veteran's Honor has a vase life of up to two weeks—an amazing length of time to remain looking fresh once cut. If for nothing else, grow this rose for cutting and arrangements.

Veteran's Honor tolerates extreme heat, has a high level of disease resistance and is easy to care for.

Whisper

Whisper was created by an Irish hybridizer named Colin Dickson. Introduced in 2003, this AARS winner is a charmer. It exhibits superior form both in the garden and in the vase. Whisper was the first white hybrid tea rose to receive the AARS designation in years, proving that a rose doesn't have to be flashy to attract attention. It exudes a light musky scent and grows best in cooler temperatures. Whisper's classically formed, creamy white blossoms will dazzle both seasoned rosarians and novice gardeners.

Other names: none
Flower color: creamy white
Flower size: 5"
Scent: slight, musk
Height: 4–5 ¹/₂'
Spread: 3–4'
Blooms: summer to fall, repeat blooming
Hardiness zones: 5–9

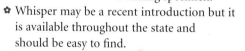

✿ This new rose bears large and long, pastel yellow buds that open into creamy white blossoms with hints of pale yellow at their centers. Each double bloom has 30–35 petals. The stiff stems are covered in semi-glossy, dark green leaves.

✿ Whisper is highly resistant to disease and requires little care.

✿ This hybrid tea has many hedging and landscape uses. Whisper's blossoms, held high on sturdy stems, seem to last forever. This makes it a good addition to a cutting garden. It can also be planted en masse or left as a stunning specimen.

✿ Whisper may be a recent introduction but it is available throughout the state and should be easy to find.

FLORIBUNDA

Floribundas are upright to free-branching bushes with prickly canes. The class was produced by crossing hybrid teas with polyanthas. They are generally smaller than hybrid teas, but have the same color range and hardiness. The clusters or sprays of small flowers bloom abundantly throughout the growing season, often smothering the foliage with blossoms. They often lack the flower form of the hybrid teas, but continued hybridization is improving the flower form. Use a floribunda in a bed or border, as a specimen, in a container or as a hedge.

Polyanthas, produced from crossing *Rosa multiflora* with *Rosa chinensis*, are the forerunners of the floribundas. These compact, free-branching bushes have sparsely prickled stems and are hardier than floribundas. Polyantha is Latin for 'many flowers,' and these roses do flower in profuse clusters. There are few polyantha varieties left in commerce as they have been superseded by the floribundas. China Doll and The Fairy are two polyanthas still common throughout the US.

Amber Queen

Other names: Prinz Eugen von Savoyen

Flower color: apricot blend

Flower size: 3–4"

Scent: sweet and spicy

Height: 2'

Spread: 2¹/₂'

Blooms: spring to fall; repeat blooming

Hardiness zones: 5–9

Amber Queen's name vividly describes its warm coloration and elegant appeal. This universally popular floribunda rose has a cushiony mound of dark, glossy foliage tinged with a copper sheen. Richly scented flowers emerge each spring in large clusters. Each plump bud opens into a cupped blossom made up of 25 to 30 petals. Amber Queen has a spreading habit and grows low to the ground, making it an ideal landscape rose. It's great for beds and borders, low hedging and containers, or for shows and exhibitions. Its long list of awards from all over the world, including the AARS award in 1988, prove this rose worthy of any garden.

✿ Amber Queen is a robust grower with a neat bedding habit. Its healthy foliage and well-formed flowers require little care or maintenance.

✿ Developed by Harkness Roses in 1984, Amber Queen was originally called Rosemary Harkness. Upon winning Britain's Rose of the Year, its name was changed for commercial acceptance.

✿ This rose is also known as Prinz Eugen von Savoyen, an 18th-century Austrian hero.

Betty Boop

This vibrant white and red floribunda was named after the famous cartoon character of the 1930s because of its perky nature and bright coloration. Bred by Tom Carruth of Weeks Roses, this recent introduction received the honorable All-American Rose Selection award in 1999. Betty Boop is almost always in bloom, bearing flowers from spring to fall frost. Each flower consists of six to twelve petals borne in clusters of three to five flowers per spray. It is a naturally rounded plant with a shrub-like density and a slight spreading habit.

Other names: Centenary of Federation

Flower color: ivory with red edges and yellow centers

Flower size: 4"

Scent: moderate, fruity

Height: 3–5'

Spread: 3–4'

Blooms: spring to fall; repeat blooming

Hardiness zones: 5–10

❀ Betty Boop is tolerant of light shade, highly resistant to disease and hardy to zone 4 with adequate winter protection.

❀ It reblooms quickly without deadheading or shaping. It is known to be a consistent grower in most climates.

❀ The long-lived flowers fade a little eventually, but remain crisp for a long time.

❀ Rounded shrub form and flowers from top to bottom make Betty Boop an ideal landscape plant. It is also suitable for use as a hedge or foundation plant. Try it in a mixed bed or border, cottage garden or en masse for impact.

Blueberry Hill

Introduced less than 10 years ago, Blueberry Hill is a new floribunda created by Tom Carruth of Weeks Roses. It is one of those special roses that brilliantly exhibits a shade of purple uncommon to most flowers. It looks powdery soft and delicate whether in bud or fully open. It is a romantic variety that will steal your heart. Floribunda means 'abundance of flowers' and this rose exemplifies the name. Large, semi-double flowers emerge atop long stems on a rounded but upright bush.

Other names: none
Flower color: mauve or lilac
Flower size: 4"
Scent: sweet apple, clove
Height: 3–4'
Spread: 2–3'
Blooms: spring to fall; repeat blooming
Hardiness zones: 5–7

❀ The flowers are ideal for cutting. A few flowers can fill a room with a glorious fragrance.
❀ The glossy foliage remains healthy throughout the season, requiring little attention.
❀ Each flower is made up of 12 to 15 petals. The flowers should be deadheaded to encourage further blooming.
❀ Blueberry Hill is almost azalea-like in spring and consistent in all climates.
❀ This rose was the result of crossing Crystalline with Playgirl. It has inherited the best characteristics of both parents, including its plump buds that open into sweetly scented blossoms.

Easy Going

Easy Going is a sport of Livin' Easy, an orange floribunda (p. 222), and has all the fine attributes of its parent. It is well known for its reliable vigor, attractive foliage and long-lasting, colorful blossoms. It bears large, cupped blooms of 30 to 40 petals each. The flowers are produced in large clusters atop a rounded growth habit. The dark, glossy foliage is especially resistant to blackspot and other typical problems that roses encounter.

* Easy Going is most effective in group plantings. The golden flowers stand out when planted in a formal border. It is also a great cut flower.
* This vigorous rose is easy to maintain.
* Easy Going was introduced by Harkness of the UK in 1996.
* The sturdy canes are often quite thick and are able to support the large clusters of long-lasting blooms.

Other names: none
Flower color: amber yellow
Flower size: 4$^1/_2$"
Scent: pleasant and fruity
Height: 3–3$^1/_2$'
Spread: 24–30"
Blooms: spring to fall; repeat blooming
Hardiness zones: 5–9

Europeana

E uropeana, a superb red rose with unfading color, is one of the most popular roses of its class for exhibition purposes. It is wonderful in the garden as well. It blooms so profusely that crimson red blossoms almost completely obscure the top of the plant. The semi-double blooms consist of 25 to 30 petals each. They open to cupped, rosette-shaped blooms produced in well-spaced, large clusters of up to 30 flowers per cluster. The young foliage emerges burgundy red and matures over time to a leathery dark bronze. It forms a compact bush of medium height, with an upright to weeping and vigorous growth habit.

Other names: none

Flower color: dark crimson red

Flower size: 3–3¹/₂"

Scent: very slight

Height: 30"–4'

Spread: 30–36"

Blooms: spring to fall; repeat blooming

Hardiness zones: 5–9

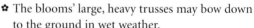

✿ This red floribunda not only tolerates intense heat but actually thrives in it, and the blooms maintain their vivid red even in the hottest flowerbeds.

✿ Europeana is stunning planted en masse or in borders. It blends well with lighter-colored flowers, especially in shades of cream and white.

✿ This rose is mildly prone to mildew but preventive measures are easy and effective. Water at the plant's base early in the morning and provide adequate air circulation. Overall, this is a relatively disease-free rose.

✿ The blooms' large, heavy trusses may bow down to the ground in wet weather.

French Lace

French Lace has everything you could possibly want in a floribunda. It is elegant and subtle in both color and fragrance, and reminiscent of roses from long ago. It has a robust nature and is very resistant to disease. French Lace was an early prototype for trendy pastel roses that continue to seduce rose gardeners today. It grew so successfully that it received the distinguished honor of the AARS in 1982. All this fuss is over a simple but elegant rose bearing large, well-formed, double flowers made up of 30 to 35 petals each. The blooms are vigorously produced in small clusters amongst small, glossy leaves in a flawless form.

Other names: none
Flower color: ivory to pale apricot
Flower size: 4¹/₂"
Scent: mild and fruity
Height: 3–5'
Spread: 2¹/₂–3'
Blooms: spring to fall; repeat blooming
Hardiness zones: 5–9

❀ The flowers are produced on thin but strong stems, ideal for cutting. Ivory roses are frequently used in a variety of arrangements but best suit tussy mussies and smaller bouquets. The petals hold their color, even when dried, making them ideal for potpourri.

❀ French Lace grows best in a location with afternoon shade.

❀ As beautiful as its parents, French Lace bears three to twelve blooms per spray.

This rose is lovely in a border or low- to medium-sized hedge. In spite of its shorter growth, the flower production is excellent and regrowth is rapid.

Hot Cocoa

Hot Cocoa is an outstanding creation, bearing flowers in eclectic color and form. Granted, roses that exhibit brown tones aren't for everyone, but they are favored among many gardeners. They are also becoming more and more popular in today's rose gardens. This rare coloration clothes each of the 25 to 30 ruffled petals that make up the fully double flowers. The flowers are large and well formed. The foliage inhabits a natural disease resistance as a result of superior breeding. Hot Cocoa was an AARS recipient in 2003. This rose is bound to be a future classic.

Other names: none

Flower color: orangy red with a brown hue

Flower size: 4"

Scent: old rose, myrrh

Height: 3½–4'

Spread: 3–4'

Blooms: spring to fall; repeat blooming

Hardiness zones: 5–9

❧ This medium-sized plant was grown across North America for two years as part of the AARS process prior to its introduction. It was judged to have exceptional qualities and results in most climates.

❧ The deep rust-colored buds open into deep chocolaty red tones that can fade slightly in hotter regions and deepen in cooler zones.

❧ The stems grow to 14–18" long, ideal for cutting and arrangements.

This rose is a must for gardeners and collectors who want something a little different.

Iceberg

Over 40 years have passed since Reimer Kordes introduced this rose into commerce, and it has stood the test of time. The shapely, rain-resistant blooms last a long time and are ideal for cutting or left on the plant to adorn a special place in the garden. The buds emerge with a touch of pink and open into well-formed, dainty, white, semi-double flowers. Each flower is made up of 30 to 35 petals in clusters of up to 15 flowers.

❀ The blooms tend to be flushed with pink when the nights are cold and damp, especially in early spring and fall. If dew or a raindrop remains on a petal in the morning, it may activate a color change and turn that part of the petal pink.

❀ This sweetly fragrant rose is ideal in mixed beds or borders, planted in large groups or left alone as a specimen. Iceberg is often grown as a tall hedge.

❀ Climbing Iceberg, a sport of Iceberg, is easily trained on small fences, pergolas, arches, pillars and veranda posts. It is considered one of the best white climbing roses available, bearing disease-resistant foliage on almost thornless stems.

❀ The lull between its bloom cycles is very short, so it appears to bloom continually and remains evergreen, reminiscent of a gardenia.

Other names: Fée des Neiges, Schneewittchen
Flower color: white
Flower size: 3–4"
Scent: strong, sweet
Height: 3–4'
Spread: 3–4'
Blooms: early to mid-spring to fall; repeat blooming
Hardiness zones: 4–9

Lady of the Dawn

Other names: none
Flower color: light pink with dark pink hints toward the petal edges
Flower size: 3–3¹/₂"
Scent: light and fruity
Height: 4–5'
Spread: 5'
Blooms: spring to fall; repeat blooming
Hardiness zones: 4–9

The matte foliage is highly resistant to disease, and little care is required to maintain this beauty.

L ady of the Dawn was introduced in 1984. Created by Ilsink in the Netherlands, this beautiful floribunda produces long, stiff shoots that tend to become weighted down by clusters of 20 or more pink blooms throughout the growing season. The soft pink flowers open like saucers to reveal gold and red stamens. Each semi-double flower is made up of ruffled petals with good substance. The arching branches grow vigorously in an upright form.

✿ Lady of the Dawn is ideal in a hedge, border or bed that requires a large rose. It's capable of growing to the height and spread of an average shrub rose. It produces long canes like a climber later in the season.
✿ Lady of the Dawn is the result of crossing INTerdress and Stat den Helder.

Lavaglut

Lavaglut was developed in 1978 by Kordes. It bears camellia-like red flowers that are so dark they almost appear black. An average of 20 to 25 petals make up each velvety blossom. The evenly spaced clusters are well maintained through summer and fall. Glossy, purplish green leaves complement ruffled, velvety flowers that last and last.

✿ Its balanced growth habit makes this rose an outstanding bedding variety. Other uses include mixed borders or hedging.

✿ Protection from blackspot may be required in areas where damp weather is common.

✿ Dark red roses can often suffer scorch in heat and wind, but Lavaglut's blooms do not.

✿ Lavaglut is sometimes confused with Intrigue, a rose bred by Warriner in 1982 that bears dark reddish purple flowers. Lavaglut is not always as readily available as the later-bred Intrigue, but it is well worth a search, as it possesses great floribunda qualities.

✿ This rose received the Royal National Rose Society Trial Ground Certificate in 1980.

Other names: Lavaglow
Flower color: dark red
Flower size: 3"
Scent: light tea
Height: 3–4'
Spread: 24"
Blooms: spring to fall; repeat blooming
Hardiness zones: 4–9

Livin' Easy

Everyone loves a rose that blooms almost continually, and this is one such rose. Livin' Easy produces well-formed buds followed by glowing blooms that retain their color very well. This rose is strong in its color class, dense and spreading in form. Its glossy foliage provides a solid base for the fully open flowers with their showy yellow stamens. It is ideal in beds or mass plantings, as a cut flower or exhibition rose.

Other names: Fellowship
Flower color: fiery apricot orange blend
Flower size: 3–4"
Scent: fruity and sweet
Height: 3–4'
Spread: 3'
Blooms: spring to fall; repeat blooming
Hardiness zones: 5–9

✿ Livin' Easy won the Royal National Rose Society Gold Medal in 1990 and was the All-America Selection in 1996.

✿ Livin' Easy lives up to its other name— Fellowship. The beautiful foliage is highly disease resistant.

✿ Many of these roses showcase pathways in London's Regent's Park. Livin' Easy has also been well used in home gardens.

Nicole

Nicole blooms prolifically in its first year. In its second year, the flower production plateaus but the blooms maintain themselves for longer periods. Showy blooms top glossy, dark green foliage. Sprays of cupped, double flowers consist of 35 petals each. The foliage grows in plentiful mounds, a little open in habit and spreading in nature. Mostly weather resistant, Nicole is a little prone to blackspot. A warmer location helps prevent the disease and intensifies the flower color.

✿ This rose can be used in containers, cutting gardens, beds and borders. With its spreading, thorny canes and growth habit, it can also work as a great barrier rose.

✿ Some people believe that Nicole, Hannah Gordon and Tabris are all the same rose and that, although they have different registered names, they were all bred by the same breeder. The three appear almost identical, with subtle differences noticeable only to keen eyes. Regardless of the confusion, if you find a specimen by any of these names, the overall coloration, growth habit and fragrance will be the same.

✿ Rosarians have appreciated Nicole's exhibition quality since 1983.

✿ This rose appears in rose competitions ranging from community contests to international shows.

Other names: Hannah Gordon, Raspberry Ice, Tabris

Flower color: soft cream; raspberry red edges

Flower size: 3"

Scent: light and sweet

Height: 3–4'

Spread: 30"

Blooms: spring to fall; repeat blooming

Hardiness zones: 5–9

Playboy

Other names: Cheerio
Flower color: yellowy orange; red edges
Flower size: 3$^{1}/_{2}$"
Scent: light apple scent
Height: 3'
Spread: 24"
Blooms: spring to fall; repeat blooming
Hardiness zones: 5–9

Playboy has been widely used in warmer climates because hot weather enhances its intense flower color. Wavy-petaled flowers appear almost single, opening from clusters of pointed buds. Each blossom displays dazzling tones of yellow blended with shades of apricot and red, and reveals beautiful bright yellow stamens. Moderately thorny canes support an abundance of dark, glossy leaves. The flowers are slightly cupped with an open form. Each semi-double flower consists of seven to ten petals in typical floribunda form.

❁ This rose truly lives up to its name; it has a smooth and charming nature and appearance.
❁ Playboy is great for hedges, mixed beds and borders, but best suits a location that begs for bright colors. This vigorous, compact yet slightly upright rose gives any garden a brilliant impact.
❁ It was introduced in 1976 by Cocker's Roses in Scotland and won the Portland Gold Medal in 1989, among many other honors.
❁ When arranged with the right combination of flowers, Playboy packs a lot of punch as a cut flower.

Purple Heart

Purple Heart resembles an antique rose but was introduced in 1999 by Tom Carruth from Weeks Roses. It falls in the 'Modern Antiques' category that refers to newly developed roses with old-fashioned appearances and scents. However, these roses are far more resistant to disease than their older counterparts. They're also more compact in habit and flower more readily and for longer periods. The magenta flowers are borne in large clusters in a cupped form. Each flower consists of 30 to 35 petals with a spicy fragrance anyone would love. Purple Heart is a sure winner, worthy of any garden setting.

Other names: none
Flower color: magenta purple
Flower size: 3¹/₂–4"
Scent: strong, spicy clove
Height: 3–4'
Spread: 3–3¹/₂'
Blooms: spring to fall; repeat blooming
Hardiness zones: 5–9

✿ Purple Heart is rounded and contained in habit. The stems are moderately clothed in prickles and healthy foliage.

✿ This rose appeals to those partial to old roses and those who simply admire its vibrant coloration and form.

✿ Purple Heart's matte green leaves, unique color and scent were inherited from its species ancestor *R. californica*, which oddly enough doesn't grow very successfully in parts of California.

✿ The flowers grow larger and more purple in cooler temperatures.

Scentimental

The name really says it all. Scentimental's striped petals are reminiscent of older heritage varieties, but this rose is new and exciting. The flowers are powerfully scented and perfect for potpourri. Its form is an improvement over its stringy ancestors. Each petal is as unique as a snowflake. Red and burgundy speckles and stripes swirl into the white petals. The flowers open quickly, exposing double flowers in large clusters made up of 25 to 30 petals each. Overall, its form, flowers and disease resistance make Scentimental worthy of its 1997 AARS designation. It was Tom Carruth's first AARS designee.

Other names: none

Flower color: burgundy red and white striped

Flower size: 4–4¹⁄₂"

Scent: intense, spicy

Height: 3–4'

Spread: 3–4'

Blooms: mid-spring to late fall; repeat blooming

Hardiness zones: 5–9

✿ This vigorous producer displays the best color and size in locations with moderate temperatures.

✿ The brightly colored blossoms have a nearly continuous repeat bloom throughout the season.

✿ The striping creates a startling visual impact in a spot that requires a little punch. Beds and borders are suitable, but Scentimental is best left as a specimen that does not take away from other plants' splendor.

Sexy Rexy

Sexy Rexy blooms considerably later than most floribundas but bears a huge first flush of blooms. It requires very little maintenance or pruning. It has a well-branched form that is dense and upright, and its thorny canes bear small, glossy, dark green foliage. Camellia-like, pale pink flowers that last for weeks are borne on the stem tips. Each flower consists of 40 or more petals. The fragrance is fresh and subtle and reminiscent of tea.

- ✿ The beautifully formed flowers sometimes bow down almost to the ground because of the weighty clusters.
- ✿ Sexy Rexy will produce an abundance of blooms a second time around after summer deadheading and trimming. When pruning, reduce the stems by up to one-half their length.
- ✿ Versatile with exhibition qualities, this rose can be used in beds, borders, massed plantings, cutting gardens or containers. It can also be grown as a standard.
- ✿ Sexy Rexy has received many awards, including the RNRS James Mason Gold Medal in 1996.
- ✿ This rose blooms vigorously and is easy to grow.

Other names:
Heckenzauber
Flower color: medium to light pink
Flower size: 3 1/2–4"
Scent: slight tea
Height: 3–4'
Spread: 30–36"
Blooms: late spring to late fall; repeat blooming
Hardiness zones: 5–11

Sheila's Perfume

Sheila's Perfume is a compact bush that tends to spread over summer in warmer climates. Showy, bicolored blooms on short stems top glossy, red-tinted, dark green foliage. The double flowers are made up of an average of 20 petals each, borne singly or in clusters.

✿ This vigorous 1985 introduction is disease resistant and weatherproof. It was bred and raised by an amateur hybridizer named Sheridan in England and has achieved international popularity. The parentage of this rose is Peer Gynt x (Daily Sketch x [Paddy McGredy x Prima Ballerina]).

✿ Sheila's Perfume bears a classically formed flower, making it ideal for a cutting garden or for borders, hedges, mixed beds or containers.

✿ It won several fragrance awards, including the Edland Fragrance Award in 1981 and the Glasgow Fragrance Award in 1989.

✿ Its name combines the name of the hybridizer's wife and the plant's most outstanding quality.

Other names: none
Flower color: pale yellow and light pink; dark pink edges
Flower size: 3½"
Scent: strong, rosy fruit
Height: 30"–3½'
Spread: 24"
Blooms: spring to fall; repeat blooming
Hardiness zones: 5–11

Simplicity

Simplicity was created by William A. Warriner from Jackson & Perkins and introduced in 1978. Owing to its upright and dense growth habit, it was originally marketed as a 'living fence' when planted in groups of 5, 10 or 15 and grown on its own roots. It was also known to bear a staggering amount of blooms. The clear, mid-pink flowers are produced in sprays in a semi-double form. Each flower consists of 18 petals. The flowers open flat from long, pointed buds saturated in fragrance.

❀ Simplicity grows tall enough for cutting and works well in a variety of fresh arrangements.
❀ It is easy to grow, resistant to disease and one of the most popular landscape roses on the market.
❀ A series of Simplicity roses ranging from red and white to yellow and purple is currently available.
❀ Simplicity received the New Zealand Gold Medal in 1976.

Other names: Pink Simplicity
Flower color: medium pink
Flower size: 3–4"
Scent: light
Height: 5'
Spread: 4–5'
Blooms: spring to fall; repeat blooming
Hardiness zones: 5–11

Sunsprite

Sunsprite is one of the best yellow floribunda roses, not only for color and habit but for fragrance as well. It won an award in Baden-Baden, Germany, in part for its outstanding scent. The flowers maintain long-lasting color without fading. The glossy foliage becomes stocky and compact over time. Sunsprite produces nicely formed, deep golden yellow blossoms on a well-behaved shrub. Its bright blooms contrast with the heavily toothed, dark foliage that ranks among the most resistant in its color class. Sunsprite is blessed with an intoxicating, sweet scent and is considered more hardy than most other yellow roses.

Other names: Friesia
Flower color: bright lemon yellow
Flower size: 3"
Scent: sweet licorice
Height: 30–36"
Spread: 24"
Blooms: mid-spring to fall; repeat blooming
Hardiness zones: 5–11

✿ Easily grown as a standard or a low, colorful hedging, it is one of the best bedding roses available.
✿ Only minimal maintenance is required, including an annual prune and adequate mulching. Deadhead to keep the plant neat and tidy.
✿ This rose is disease resistant and vigorous.
✿ A new climbing form of Sunsprite is best used on arbors and trellises.
✿ Sunsprite is also called Friesia, after the province in Germany where it originated in 1977.

Trumpeter

Trumpeter was named in reference to Louis Armstrong, in whose honor the seed parent Satchmo was also named. Presumably the breeder, Sam McGredy IV, is a fan of this musical genius. It's not unfair to say that this rose's appeal compares to Mr. Armstrong's talent; both are stunning and inspiring. It bears loosely cupped blossoms in a double form consisting of 35 to 40 petals each. The large flowers have ruffled red-orange petals and medium green, glossy foliage. Bushy and compact, this vigorous rose grows into a neat and upright form. It blooms in such abundance that the branches can bow down to the ground from the weight of the flower clusters.

Other names: none
Flower color: scarlet red with hints of orange
Flower size: 3¹/₂"
Scent: slight
Height: 2–3'
Spread: 2–3'
Blooms: spring to fall; repeat blooming
Hardiness zones: 5–9

✿ Trumpeter can withstand all kinds of weather with no adverse affects. It requires little care and likes a lot of heat.
✿ The long-lasting, brightly colored blooms are well suited to mass plantings, low hedging, containers and beds. It is also frequently grown for exhibition purposes or as a standard.
✿ The petals fall to the ground once spent, and its only drawback is its light scent.
✿ This popular landscape rose won a number of awards, including the Royal National Rose Society Gold Medal in 1991.

GRANDIFLORA

The grandiflora class was created in 1954 to accommodate a new rose—Queen Elizabeth (page 238)—which didn't easily fit into any other existing class. This class arose from crossing hybrid teas and floribundas.

There is some controversy about the name of this cluster-flowered class. North Americans call this class grandiflora, while the British call it floribunda, hybrid tea type. These roses are tall, upright, vigorous growers with several small stems arising from the main canes. Each cane has flowers growing singly or in small clusters, with each stem long enough for cutting. The flowers are similar to, but usually smaller than, hybrid teas and are borne in larger quantities. Some varieties are hard to distinguish from hybrid teas. Use grandifloras in the same way as hybrid teas, but prune them like floribundas.

Cherry Parfait

Other names: none
Flower color: creamy white edged in red
Flower size: 3¹/₂–4"
Scent: light
Height: 4–5'
Spread: 4'
Blooms: spring to fall; repeat blooming
Hardiness zones: 5–9

Cherry Parfait is a stunning creation of Meilland Roses from France. It was introduced in 2003 and received the AARS designation the same year. It is considered one of the most impressive landscape roses to come along in years. This grandiflora is almost shrubby but it works as a background thanks to its very showy and colorful flowers. Each fully double flower is made up of 30 to 35 petals that open from pointed, medium-sized buds. There are two to five blooms per stem atop this rounded, dense plant. Each creamy white petal is edged in striking red.

✿ Highly disease resistant, Cherry Parfait offers loads of color in all climates.
✿ Its loose growth habit makes it the perfect companion for perennials and other shrubbery. It would do well in a country garden setting or a mixed bed or border.
✿ The deep, dark green foliage is clean and healthy.
✿ Cherry Parfait is the result of crossing Jacqueline Nebout with Tamango and Matangi.

Gold Medal

As the buds emerge in spring, their outer petals suffused with pink tones, you could be fooled into thinking that Gold Medal may produce pink blossoms. As the buds unfurl, however, the yellow shines through. The flowers have a classic rose appearance in a double form, with 30 to 35 petals each. The flowers are mostly borne singly, but they're also carried on open trusses. Each flower has a high center and reflexed outer petals. A fruity aroma emanates from the large blossoms all season long. Gold Medal was considered the best rose of the 1980s and it remains popular in commerce today.

Other names: Aroyqueli

Flower color: yellow with hints of pink on the undersides and upper edges

Flower size: 4¹/₂–5"

Scent: slight, fruity

Height: 3–4'

Spread: 2–3'

Blooms: spring to fall; repeat blooming

Hardiness zones: 5–9

* This hardy rose is nicely shaped and won't mind if it's pruned too low. You'll be rewarded with copious blooms if it's allowed to grow taller.
* Gold Medal is a fine landscape rose that's great for cutting and arrangements. The prolific blooming cycle will enable you to keep a vase full of freshly cut flowers all season long.
* It is usually one of the last roses to bloom each growing season, but it is well worth the wait. It tends to fill in the gaps while other roses are resting between cycles.
* Gold Medal vigorously produces a constant supply of flowers atop a tall and upright plant with bushy growth and an exhibition form.
* It was introduced in 1982 and bred by Jack E. Christensen.

Love

This rose was part of a group of roses developed in 1980 by William A. Warriner of the US. It was released along with Honor and Cherish, and all three received the All-America Rose Selection designation the same year. Some classify Love as a hybrid tea, while others consider it a grandiflora. Either way, it is one of the most stunning roses ever developed. The dull buds open slowly into tightly packed, high-centered, double blooms. Each scarlet petal's reverse is bright silvery white and is well displayed when the blooms first begin to unfurl. The brightness eventually disappears as the cupped form takes shape. The thorny stems bear sparse foliage.

Other names: none
Flower color: scarlet red with silvery white reverse
Flower size: 3½"
Scent: light and spicy
Height: 3–4'
Spread: 30"
Blooms: spring to fall; repeat blooming
Hardiness zones: 5–10

✿ Love has a stocky form thanks to its moderately vigorous branches. It tends to spread over time, but not in an aggressive manner. The foliage is moderately resistant to disease but mildly susceptible to blackspot.

✿ The weight of the blooms will sometimes cause the stems to bow down to the ground.

✿ Dark pink and silver bicolored roses are rare, but this variety is certainly the best of the few that exist. It received the Portland Gold Medal in 1980.

Melody Parfumée

Its name is a good indicator of what you're in for when you plant Melody Parfumée in your garden. It is intensely scented and reminiscent of old damask roses. The flowers are lovely and open flat as they age to display golden yellow stamens surrounded by 26 to 40 petals. The flowers are borne in large clusters in a double, urn-shaped form with tight centers. This all takes place on straight stems covered in bluish green, semi-glossy foliage. It was bred by Dorieux from France in 1995.

✿ This upright and bushy rose has won three awards since its introduction.

✿ The long stems are ideal for cutting, and the flowers blend well with a variety of other flowers for fresh and dried arrangements. The powerful scent will instantly fill a room with an intoxicating fragrance.

✿ This rose is a bit of a late bloomer, beginning shortly after others complete their first flush.

Other names: Violette Parfumeé

Flower color: dark lavender plum with a lighter reverse

Flower size: 4¹/₂"

Scent: intense, damask

Height: 4–5'

Spread: 3–4'

Blooms: spring to fall; repeat blooming

Hardiness zones: 5–10

Queen Elizabeth

This rose was introduced in 1954, an important year for roses. Queen Elizabeth was unique among roses, so the grandiflora classification was created to accommodate it. It is one of the most widely grown and best-loved roses and has received many honors, including being named World's Favorite Rose in 1979. It bears large, double, high-centered, medium pink flowers singly or in clusters. Each flower consists of 35 to 40 petals in a cupped form. The dark, glossy foliage is highly resistant to disease.

Other names: The Queen Elizabeth Rose, Queen of England
Flower color: medium pink
Flower size: 3¹⁄₂–4"
Scent: light tea
Height: 4¹⁄₂–6'
Spread: 30–36"
Blooms: spring to fall; repeat blooming
Hardiness zones: 4–9

❀ This trouble-free rose is ideal for hedging and works well at the back of borders and planters. It thrives in the worst conditions and can endure extreme heat, humidity or a bout with insects with very little assistance.

❀ Prune it back quite hard every six years or so to rejuvenate it and allow the shrub to become more compact and dense. The flowers will then bloom at eye level so you can enjoy them.

❀ Long, sturdy stems make it easy to cut and display the infinitely rewarding blooms.

Tournament of Roses

Tournament of Roses is one of those roses that fit into a variety of classifications. It is considered a grandiflora in North America but a hybrid tea elsewhere. The double, high-centered flowers have an excellent continuity of bloom throughout summer into fall. Three to six flowers form a symmetrical cluster. Each flower has 35 to 40 petals, and the petals are varying shades of pink.

* Although this beautiful rose is easy to grow, it has some drawbacks. Some growers think it is too small, and it has only average to moderate vigor.
* Tournament of Roses blends easily into mixed beds and borders, and is a good variety for hedging and group plantings. It is one of the best grandifloras for display and exhibition. The flower color is particularly spectacular in warm weather.
* The name refers to the annual rose parade held in Pasadena, California. This rose was released for public sale on the parade's centenary.

Other names: Berkeley, Poesie
Flower color: medium coral pink
Flower size: 3½–4"
Scent: light and spicy
Height: 36"
Spread: 36"
Blooms: spring to fall; repeat blooming
Hardiness zones: 4–9

MINIATURE

Miniature roses are small and sparsely prickly, and usually grown on their own roots. Miniatures were very popular in the early 19th century when the first miniatures, cultivars of *Rosa chinensis* 'Minima,' were produced in abundance. Their popularity waned with the introduction of the polyantha roses. Interest in miniatures was rekindled when Dr. Roulet found a China rose growing in a window box in a Swiss village. This small rose was called Rouletii, and many miniature varieties were bred from it.

Most of the modern miniature roses were developed from the breeding program of Ralph Moore in Visalia, California. Some newer varieties arise from other than miniature parents. These popular roses look like their bigger relatives—the hybrid teas and floribundas—but they are smaller, usually less than 18" tall. They bear tiny flowers and foliage.

Miniature roses are ideal for edging beds and borders, raised beds, planters or rock gardens, window boxes or for use indoors as short-term houseplants. Climbing and trailing miniatures, a result of crossing miniatures with *Rosa wichuraiana*, are also available. Patio roses, another type of miniature rose, are slightly larger than miniatures and resemble floribundas. Another type has been introduced that bears flowers slightly larger than miniatures but smaller than floribundas. They are called mini-flora. Miniatures require consistent deadheading for the best display of blooms.

Cupcake

Cupcake exibits strong, healthy growth and blooms throughout the season. This relatively thornless variety has the traditional characteristics of a high-centered, large-flowered modern rose, but in miniature. Small clusters of uncluttered, pointed, pink petals encircle bright yellow stamens. Each flower consists of at least 60 neatly overlapping petals. The florets are produced in small clusters of one to five blooms. The glossy, neat, rounded foliage is highly disease resistant.

Other names: none
Flower color: clear pale pink
Flower size: 1½"
Scent: mild to none
Height: 12–18"
Spread: 12–14"
Blooms: early spring to fall; repeat blooming
Hardiness zones: 5–11

✿ Cupcake is ideal for growing in containers, as low hedging or as a groundcover.
✿ This undemanding and virtually maintenance-free rose was created by Mark C. Spies in 1981.
✿ Cupcake won the 1983 American Rose Society Award of Excellence, and it is one of the few miniature roses created by an amateur hybridizer to win this award.
✿ Cupcake can be brought indoors for short periods of time for a burst of color.
✿ Remove the spent flowers to keep the plant tidy and encourage further blooming.

Fairhope

Fairhope is an exhibition-style rose, bearing elegant blossoms in a miniature form. Their color and shape hold well, and the foliage stands up to disease. The flowers are borne in abundance in near white to pale yellow. The 16 to 28 petals come together in a high-centered double form from pointed buds. The straight stems are covered in medium red prickles and glossy foliage. The scent is subtle and light and doesn't contradict the delicate appearance of this little beauty.

✿ The flowers are followed by small, rounded green fruit, or hips, in the fall. These hips further embellish this miniature well into winter.

✿ Fairhope is a must for showing and exhibition. It is considered the nation's top show rose and is ideal for any garden setting.

✿ The flowers are beautiful in fresh arrangements and are often used in boutonnieres and tussy mussies.

✿ Introduced in 1989 by Pete and Kay Taylor of Taylor's Roses, Fairhope was named after the breeders' lovely bayside community in Alabama. It is considered one of the top 25 miniature roses available today.

Other names: none
Flower color: pastel yellow
Flower size: 3"
Scent: slight
Height: 2–2¹/₂'
Spread: 2–2¹/₂'
Blooms: spring to fall; repeat blooming
Hardiness zones: 5–9

Giggles

Giggles is nothing to laugh at. With an exquisite form similar to that of a hybrid tea, Giggles often takes top prize at exhibition shows. The long stems support tiny, medium pink blossoms with a creamy pink reverse. A hint of peach in the petals contrasts beautifully with the light to medium matte foliage. Each lightly scented flower is made up of 20 to 25 petals unfurling evenly from a high center. The overall form is upright and bushy and the flowers emerge on long, strong canes with white thorns. The flowers are borne profusely all season long.

Other names: none
Flower color: medium pink
Flower size: 3"
Scent: slight
Height: 2–2¹/₂'
Spread: 2–2¹/₂'
Blooms: spring to fall; repeat blooming
Hardiness zones: 5–9

The foliage is disease resistant and winter hardy.

❀ Giggles is an excellent garden performer. It requires little care and doesn't need to be coddled.

❀ Almost every rose has an official registered code name. The Giggles described here has the code name KINgig, which differentiates it from another pink miniature rose called Giggles with the code name LYOgi. They were bred by different people in different years. The rose we recommend was bred by Benson E. 'Gene' King of the US in 1987. It was introduced by AGM Miniature Roses and resulted from crossing Vera Dalton and Rose Window.

Gizmo

Gizmo is a cute name for an adorable rose. It was bred in 2000 by Tom Carruth of Weeks Roses. This newcomer is a complete package of color, form, disease resistance and fragrance. The large, single blooms are made up of 4 to 11 petals in a striking blend of scarlet red and orange. Each flower has a central white eye surrounding the bright yellow stamens. Small clusters of flowers sit atop the semi-glossy, dark foliage. Gizmo grows into a mound-like, compact form. The scent is unforgettable and as unique as the color itself.

Other names: Cal Trans
Flower color: scarlet orange with a white eye
Flower size: 1–2"
Scent: mild apple
Height: 1–2'
Spread: 1–2'
Blooms: late spring to fall; repeat blooming
Hardiness zones: 5–10

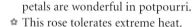 The flowers are not only beautiful but long lived and ideal for cutting. A prolific bloomer, Gizmo will provide you with flowers for cutting all season long.

❀ This rose is a consistent grower in all climates and its disease resistance is second to none.

❀ Gizmo vigorously produces a dense thicket of foliage on nicely branched, short stems, ideal for hedging or a low border. This form is beautifully displayed in containers on a sunny deck, along the front of mixed beds and borders or in a cutting garden for arrangements and crafts. The petals are wonderful in potpourri.

❀ This rose tolerates extreme heat.

Glowing Amber

In its short life, Glowing Amber has won awards from around the globe, a remarkable feat on the part of hybridizer George Mander, who developed this miniature beauty in 1996. This extraordinary rose exhibits a flawless form in shades of red to yellow. The classic hybrid tea-formed blossoms are velvety red with a vibrant yellow reverse. The balanced flowers are made up of 26 to 40 petals each, often emerging one flower to a stem. The dark, glossy foliage beautifully complements the bright flowers.

❀ This upright, prolific bloomer has straight stems long enough for cutting. The fiery shades look great in fresh arrangements with a variety of perennials and annuals.

❀ Glowing Amber is easy to grow and has enormous exhibition potential; it is ranked as one of the top 10 miniature roses for exhibition. It is also ideal as a garden rose for traditional or contemporary settings.

❀ The blossoms are resistant to rain and extreme weather and can tolerate dappled shade. Glowing Amber is highly disease resistant.

❀ George Mander is one of North America's leading amateur rose hybridizers. Known within rose circles throughout the world, he continues to create new crosses from his home in British Columbia, Canada.

Other names: none
Flower color: scarlet red; yellow reverse
Flower size: 2–2$\frac{1}{2}$"
Scent: mild
Height: 1$\frac{1}{2}$–2$\frac{1}{2}$'
Spread: 1–2'
Bloom period: summer to fall; repeat blooming
Hardiness zones: 5–9

Gourmet Popcorn

Gourmet Popcorn is a sport of Popcorn and has similar characteristics but a few unique traits as well. It bears cascading clusters of rounded, white, semi-double flowers with short stems. Each flower consists of 6 to 14 petals and is borne in large clusters of 30 to 60 flowers. The flowers are complemented by deep green, lush foliage. Gourmet Popcorn vigorously forms into a compact, cushion-like, rounded shrub. It really is more of a small shrub than a miniature rose.

✿ This rose is stunning planted en masse or in pots, containers, hanging baskets or any small spaces that need a boost. Gourmet Popcorn emits a distinctive honey scent. Plant this rose where the fragrance can be best enjoyed—alongside pathways, under windows or next to a garden bench.

✿ It is highly resistant to disease and virtually maintenance free.

✿ In warmer regions, Gourmet Popcorn can grow up to twice its typical height, creating a stunning specimen bearing hundreds of flowers at a time.

✿ Introduced in the US in 1988 by Luis Desamero, this rose won the RNRS Trial Ground Certificate in 1995.

Other names: none
Flower color: white
Flower size: $^3/_4$"
Scent: honey
Height: 18–24"
Spread: 24"
Blooms: spring to fall; repeat blooming
Hardiness zones: 4–9

Green Ice

Other names: none

Flower color: white, hints of pink and chartreuse

Flower size: 1¼"

Scent: slight

Height: 8–16"

Spread: 16–24"

Blooms: mid-spring to late summer; repeat blooming

Hardiness zones: 5–11

The unique flower color of Green Ice is its most outstanding characteristic. Pinkish buds emerge in spring and open to double, white blooms touched with a hint of pink. The flowers then change to a light chartreuse green as they age. Green Ice is a vigorous, low-growing dwarf shrub with a spreading form. It can be trained as a tiny climber in the right location. Glossy, dark green foliage is produced on short, lax stems. It bears hundreds of flowers during the first bloom cycle.

✿ Green Ice will cascade over rock walls and embankments. It is suitable for hanging baskets, edging or borders and blends nicely in larger garden settings. Some people think it resembles an old garden rose, with its double, pompom-like blooms.

✿ Green Ice is generally disease resistant but requires good air circulation and regular feeding to prevent powdery mildew.

✿ This variety was introduced in 1971 by Ralph S. Moore of the US.

✿ The blooms' color intensity is greatly affected by light levels. The flowers have a deeper green tone in partial shade and fade to white with a hint of green in full sun.

Hot Tamale

Hot Tamale bears extraordinary flowers that transform from one color to another. When they first emerge, the flowers are a striking yellow-orange blend. Over time a vibrant pink slightly obscures the yellow coloring until finally the three colors merge in an electric glow unique to this rose. Hot Tamale wins show after show with its exhibition form and unique color. The flower color lasts and lasts against the dark, semi-glossy foliage. Hot Tamale is a little flower factory, producing wave after wave of blooms when planted in full sun with routine fertilizing and ample water.

- This tiny rose has a bushy and compact form. The stout canes are covered with dense, healthy foliage and few prickles. It can survive in zone 4 with adequate winter protection.
- It was bred by Dr. Keith W. Zary of the US in 1993. The year following its introduction it won the ARS Award of Excellence, an honor reserved for the best.

Other names: Sunbird
Flower color: yellow, pink and orange blend
Flower size: 1^1/$_2$–2"
Scent: slight, sweet
Height: 18–22"
Spread: 24–28"
Blooms: summer to fall; repeat blooming
Hardiness zones: 5–11

Hot Tamale bears flowers with perfect hybrid tea form, but in miniature.

Incognito

Other names: none
Flower color: mauve blend with yellow reverse
Flower size: 1"
Scent: slight to none
Height: 1–3'
Spread: 1–2'
Blooms: spring to fall; repeat blooming
Hardiness zones: 6–10

It received the prestigious honor of winning the New England Rose Trials in 1996.

This miniature has no reason for a disguise. Incognito is an eclectic mix of mauve and yellow. Its tiny double flowers, borne mostly singly on straight stems, are made up of 15 to 25 petals. The petals have excellent substance and come together in an exhibition form. The blooms openly quickly to reveal their unique coloration and continue to do so all season long. Semi-glossy, dark foliage is untouched by disease and grows on prickly stems covered by bushy growth.

✿ Incognito is often grown for exhibition and show purposes but you don't have to be a rosarian to grow this miniature. Its appeal has increased since it was introduced in 1995.

✿ The result of crossing Jean Kenneally with Twilight Trail, Incognito was bred by Dennis Bridges of Bridges Roses in the US.

✿ Incognito is one of those roses you have to grow just for the color combination. It is one of the all-time best miniatures.

Irresistible

Irresistible is another aptly named miniature rose. Who doesn't love tiny white flowers with pale pink centers and a hint of green? It is a sure winner among those who are passionate about miniatures. Tiny buds open into medium-sized blossoms made up of 40 to 45 petals in an exhibition form. The spicy-scented flowers are borne singly and in small clusters. Globular, yellow-brown fruit follows the flowers at season's end. The strong canes are clothed in yellow and red, straight prickles and medium green, semi-glossy foliage. Irresistible has an upright, tall form for a miniature and has been known to grow up to 3' tall.

❀ The blooms are known to last for days when cut and for weeks on the bush. Rumor has it an Irresistible bloom that won Queen of Show was exhibited a week later and nearly won Queen again—simply unheard of and testament to the flowers' longevity!

❀ Irresistible has won an alarming number of awards, and it has even beat out its creator's previous masterpiece, Jean Kenneally. Introduced in 1990, this mini became an instant hit, winning just about every competition it entered.

❀ Irresistible was bred by the late Cecilia 'Dee' Bennett in 1989 and introduced by Tiny Petals Nursery the following year. It was the result of crossing Tiki and Brian Lee.

Other names: none
Flower color: white with pale pink center
Flower size: 3/4–1 1/4"
Scent: moderate, spicy
Height: 24–36"
Spread: 24–36"
Blooms: spring to fall; repeat blooming
Hardiness zones: 5–9

The color can vary a little depending on climate and growing conditions.

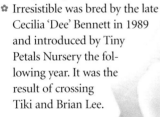

Jean Kenneally

Other names: none
Flower color: pale apricot blend
Flower size: 1¹⁄₂–2"
Scent: light
Height: 2–3'
Spread: 2'
Blooms: late spring to fall; repeat blooming
Hardiness zones: 5–10

Jean Kenneally is one of the most famous miniature roses ever created, and for good reason. With its unsurpassed beauty, it's a sure winner among rosarians and everyday gardeners. The small, double flowers exhibit great form in large clusters of 10 to 12. Twenty-two pale apricot petals make up each blossom, which can also be found singly. Jean Kenneally can produce up to 100 to 150 perfect show blooms at one time, something that few miniature roses can do. Named after a Southern Californian rosarian, this rose won more than 400 royalty awards in its first year alone. At only 20 years old it remains one of the ARS' highest-rated miniature roses, and it received a higher rating than any hybrid tea on record.

❀ This mini produces long stems that tower over other miniature rose shrubs. It boasts clean, unblemished foliage, superb form and classic blooms.

❀ A slight pink tinge may develop on the petals in cooler climates.

❀ Its upright habit has been known to surpass its standard 2–3' height in various regions throughout the US. Growers have even reported heights up to 6'.

❀ Great for cutting and arrangements, this rose is considered one of the best miniatures used by florists and exhibitors across the country.

❀ Jean Kenneally was bred by the late Dee Bennett of Tiny Petals Nursery in 1984.

Magic Carrousel

Magic Carrousel is an ARS Miniature Rose Hall of Fame recipient, created by Ralph Moore. It has won the hearts of exhibitors and gardeners since its introduction in 1972. It produces a constant display of gorgeous, long-stemmed, pure white blooms with a picotee edge of deep pink to red. This vigorous miniature can bear hundreds of flawless blooms in one season. Each fully double flower is lightly scented and displays a striking and unique color combination. Its popularity hasn't waned since its introduction, and it will likely be a classic for future generations.

Other names: Magic Carrousel

Flower color: white-edged red

Flower size: 1–1½"

Scent: slight

Height: 18–24"

Spread: 12–18"

Blooms: spring to fall; repeat blooming

Hardiness zones: 6–10

✿ The flowers are at their best when fully open, with a hint of yellow surrounding the bright yellow stamens exposed for all to see. The healthy foliage contrasts beautifully with the deep pinky red and crisp white petals.

✿ Magic Carrousel received the American Rose Society Award of Excellence in 1975 as well as the Hall of Fame designation. This mini holds a cherished place in miniature rose history as one of the first varieties to receive this status.

The flowers are ideal for garnishing a wreath or a cake when picked in bud or just after the flower has opened.

Minnie Pearl

Other names: none
Flower color: light pink with a yellow base
Flower size: 1¹/₂"
Scent: slight
Height: 14–20"
Spread: 14–20"
Blooms: mid-spring to fall; repeat blooming
Hardiness zones: 5–10

The character of Minnie Pearl on the television program *Hee Haw* was dubbed the 'Queen of Country Comedy,' famous for her trademark 'Howdy!' Sarah Cannon, the actress who played Minnie, spoke of her alter ego and the connection to her fans when she said, 'The price tag on my hat seems to be symbolic of all human frailty. There's old Minnie standing on stage in her best dress, telling everybody how proud she is to be there, and she's forgotten to take the $1.98 price tag off her hat.' A beautiful and lasting tribute to the character, this rose has country appeal, with soft pink tones touched with darker pink hues and a soft yellow base.

✿ The long, elegant buds unfurl evenly from a high center. The flowers, made up of at least 35 petals each and reminiscent of tiny hybrid tea blossoms, are produced among small, semi-glossy foliage in a rounded form.

✿ The flower color tends to darken in hot sun.

✿ Minnie Pearl bears enough flowers to cut for arrangements. The blooms are easily spotted by rain; deadhead to replace damaged flowers.

✿ Minnie Pearl produces exhibition-quality blooms. It is an upright and well-shaped bush suitable for any garden setting. It looks adorable along the front of borders and beds in a country garden setting. It is also effective grouped in containers.

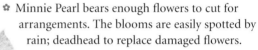

Miss Flippins

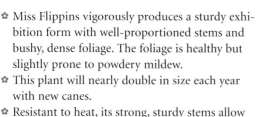

Miss Flippins is an elegant little miniature rose that produces long-stemmed buds early in the summer months. The buds unfurl to reveal classically formed double flowers that resemble hybrid tea blooms. Each flower is made up of 15 to 25 red petals with a pink reverse. Medium-sized dark and glossy foliage blends beautifully with the colorful flowers. Robbie Tucker of Bridges Roses created this rose and released it for introduction in 1997. Miss Flippins is a relative newcomer with a bright future.

Other names: none
Flower color: medium red with a deep pink reverse
Flower size: 1½–2"
Scent: none
Height: 2–2½'
Spread: 2'
Blooms: summer to fall; repeat blooming
Hardiness zones: 5–9

✿ Miss Flippins vigorously produces a sturdy exhibition form with well-proportioned stems and bushy, dense foliage. The foliage is healthy but slightly prone to powdery mildew.

✿ This plant will nearly double in size each year with new canes.

✿ Resistant to heat, its strong, sturdy stems allow for cutting and display within the home or on the show table.

✿ Miss Flippins has been known to win numerous competitions but is a reliable, prolific garden rose as well.

Pierrine

Pierrine is another miniature worth showing off, whether it's in your home, garden or at the local rose society show. Either way, Pierrine bears dainty, double flowers slightly larger than the average miniature. They're mostly borne singly, made up of 40 delicate petals each. The fragrance couldn't be better matched, as a pink rose most suits a subtle damask scent. Pierrine was created by Michael C. William and introduced in 1988. A result of crossing Tiki and Party Girl, this rose would suit any level of gardener and works well in a number of settings.

Other names: none
Flower color: medium pink with a slightly lighter reverse
Flower size: 2¹⁄₂–3"
Scent: slight, damask
Height: 2¹⁄₂'
Spread: 2'
Blooms: summer to fall; repeat blooming
Hardiness zones: 5–9

✿ Tiny, round fruit follow the flowers in shades of green and orange. This lengthens the seasonal color long after the flowers have taken their bow.
✿ Tall stems carry healthy foliage with downcurved prickles and semi-glossy foliage with serrated edges. Pierrine grows into an upright form.
✿ Pierrine is frequently used in shows by collectors and rosarians from one coast to the other.

Rainbow's End

Rainbow's End is considered one of the most beautiful miniature roses ever created and is ranked the most popular miniature available today. It bears pointed buds that open into double, classic hybrid tea-type blooms in deep yellow shades touched with dark pinky red. The pinky red color will intensify in full sun, creating a distinctive edge. Age can also influence the intensity, and the entire petal may turn almost completely red. Sturdy, maroon stems support small, dark, glossy leaves with burgundy, serrated edges. This rose has a rounded and compact, well-branched and upright form.

❀ Generally resistant to disease, this rose is a little prone to blackspot.

❀ With its bushy and upright form, Rainbow's End works best in the garden. It is suitable for cut-flower gardens, beds or borders. It also works in containers or as an indoor plant in winter.

❀ Introduced in 1984, Rainbow's End received the ARS Award of Excellence in 1986. A climbing variety has since been introduced.

Other names: none

Flower color: deep yellow; dark pinky red edges

Flower size: 1¹/₂"

Scent: mild to none

Height: 12–16"

Spread: 10–14"

Blooms: early spring to fall; repeat blooming

Hardiness zones: 4–11

Rise 'n' Shine

Rise 'n' Shine has been a favorite of gardeners for over 25 years, and for good reason. As a yellow rose, it is hard to beat. It bears uniquely formed quill-like petals, with about 30 or 40 petals per flower. The flowers exhibit hybrid tea form in rosette clusters. Deadheading is a must to encourage a continuous flush of flowers throughout summer.

Other names: Golden Sunblaze
Flower color: brilliant yellow
Flower size: $1^{1}/_{2}$–$1^{3}/_{4}$"
Scent: slight, fruity
Height: 16–20"
Spread: 12–14"
Blooms: summer to fall; repeat blooming
Hardiness zones: 5–10

❀ Though generally resistant to disease, Rise 'n' Shine is slightly prone to blackspot and powdery mildew. Plant it in a sunny location with good air circulation. This mini tolerates extreme heat and is great for cutting. It can also be grown successfully in zone 4 with sufficient winter protection.

❀ Rise 'n' Shine is well suited to beds, borders, edgings and container plantings. It is also a popular show variety.

❀ This rose is one of the finest yellow miniatures and is outstanding in its color class. It received the ARS Award of Excellence in 1978, and in 1999 it was one of the first inductees into the Miniature Rose Hall of Fame.

❀ It was hybridized by Ralph S. Moore of the US, who is known as the greatest miniature rose breeder to date.

Snow Bride

Snow Bride is a nicely rounded shrub and one of the best white miniatures with a hybrid tea form. It is not a rose for people who tend to neglect their plants—if not tended to, it will fail or become unsightly. Unlike most white miniature roses, this one produces beautiful white, weatherproof flowers. The flowers tend to be twice as large as those of other miniature varieties. The buds open into circular blossoms with pointed centers, made up of 20 petals. Small, dark, glossy leaves complement the bright blossoms.

✿ This rose is suitable for containers, borders or along the edges of mixed beds. It prefers partial shade and moderate temperatures.

✿ Snow Bride was introduced in 1982 and won the ARS Award of Excellence for Miniature Roses only one year later. It was bred by Betty J. Jolly in the US.

Other names:
Snowbride
Flower color: white
Flower size: 1¹/₂–2"
Scent: slight
Height: 12–16"
Spread: 12–16"
Blooms: mid-spring to fall; repeat blooming
Hardiness zones: 4–10

Starina

Rated highly by the ARS, Starina has proven to be a consistent performer within its class. It has won a number of prestigious awards and its popularity hasn't waned since its introduction in 1965. Early in the season it produces pointed buds that open into well-formed flowers made up of 30 to 35 petals. The fully double flowers resemble a hybrid tea form, borne singly and in small clusters. Its dark, glossy foliage is unaffected by disease. Meilland Roses raised the bar when they created Starina, which is considered the 'Peace' of the miniatures.

Other names: none
Flower color: deep reddish orange
Flower size: 1"
Scent: slight
Height: 12–18"
Spread: 12–18"
Blooms: late spring to fall; repeat blooming
Hardiness zones: 5–10

✿ Easy to grow, Starina requires little care and maintenance. It's hard to beat its rounded form, dwarf growth and warm red colors.

✿ Starina is a consistent grower in all climates.

✿ It is an excellent rose to grow for cutting and arrangements, in beds, borders and containers on a sunny patio.

✿ Starina won awards from around the world, including the Japan Gold Medal in 1968 and the Anerkannte Deutsche Rose award in 1971.

Winsome

Winsome is a vigorous producer and proven performer with a free-flowering habit. It blooms in shades of purple rarely found in roses. The big, pointed buds open into large, shapely blooms. The fully double flowers consist of 35 to 40 petals surrounding bright gold stamens. Borne singly or in long-stemmed clusters, this mini-flora rose is a beautiful addition to flower beds, borders and especially containers. Winsome was created in 1985 by Harmon F. Saville, who founded Nor'East Miniature roses in 1971 in his backyard. His son once said that Harmon 'liked to describe his business as a hobby gone wild, as his interests increased from growing minis to marketing them and ultimately hybridizing.' Winsome remains popular and is destined to become a miniature classic.

✿ Colorful blossoms and long, sturdy stems lend perfectly to cutting and arrangements.
✿ Winsome's flower color doesn't fade and the flowers last and last. Spent blooms fall off by themselves before the next cycle begins.
✿ The blooms grow larger in cooler climates. The shading becomes darker as well, making the colorful blossoms even more attractive.
✿ The dark, semi-glossy foliage is resistant to disease and remains unblemished throughout the season.

Other names: none
Flower color: deep magenta with a red tinge
Flower size: 1"
Scent: little to none
Height: 16–22"
Spread: 16–22"
Blooms: early summer to fall; repeat blooming
Hardiness zones: 5–10

Resources

Gardens to Visit

Auburn Area Chamber of Commerce Rose Gardens
601 Lincoln Way
Auburn, CA 95603
530-888-5616
www.geocities.com/Rain Forest/Wetlands/1395/publicgardens.html

Berkeley Municipal Rose Gardens
Euclid Avenue between Bay View Place and Eunice Street
Berkeley, CA 94704
510-644-6530
www.ci.berkeley.ca.us/manager/news/roses.htm

Capitol Park Rose Garden
1300 L Street
Sacramento, CA 95814
916-445-3658
www.capitolmuseum.ca.gov/virtualtours/park/html/stop6/

Elizabeth F. Gamble Garden
1431 Waverley Street
Palo Alto, CA 94301
650-329-1356
www.gamblegarden.org

Filoli Gardens
86 Cañada Road
Woodside, CA 94062
650-364-8300 ext. 507
www.filoli.org

Fountain Square Rose Garden
6237 Fountain Square Drive
Citrus Heights, CA 95621-5577
916-240-6631

Garden Valley Ranch Nursery
498 Pepper Road
Petaluma, CA 94952
707-795-0919
www.gardenvalley.com

Golden Gate Park Rose Garden
Golden Gate Park, Section 7
San Francisco, CA 94117
415-666-7003
www.mistersf.com/high/index.html?highrose.htm

Los Altos Redwood Grove Nature Preserve
482 University Avenue
Los Altos, CA
650-947-2790 or 650-917-0342

McKinley Park Rose Garden
601 Alhambra Boulevard
Sacramento, CA 95816
916-264-7316 or 916-277-6060

Morcom Rose Gardens
700 Jean Street
Oakland, CA 94610
510-238-3187
www.oakland.com/parks/facilities/rental_morcom.asp

Rengstorff House
Shoreline at Mountain View
Shoreline Boulevard off Highway 101
650-903-6392 (administration) or 650-903-6088 (Rengstorff House)
www.ci.mtnview.ca.us/city-depts/cs/shoreline.htm
www.r-house.org/

San Jose Municipal Rose Garden
Naglee and Dana Avenue
San Jose, CA
408-277-5561
www.ci.san-jose.ca.us/cae/parkss/rg/

Santa Clara University Mission Rose Garden
820 Alviso Street
Santa Clara, CA 95050
408-554-4000
info@scu.edu

Strybing Arboretum and Botanical Gardens
Golden Gate Park
9th Avenue and Lincoln Way
San Francisco, CA
415-661-1316
www.strybing.org

Rose Societies & Clubs

American Rose Society
PO Box 30,000
Shreveport, LA 1130-0030
318-938-5402
www.ars.org

Northern California–Nevada–Hawaii District
ARS
776 Pinedale Ct.
Hayward, CA 94544-1025
www.ncnhdistrict.org

Butte Rose Society
Chico–Paradise
530-342-5045

Central Valley Rose Society
Stockton–Modesto
209-931-8175

www.geocities.com/cvros-esociety/

Contra Costa Rose Society
Contra Costa County
925-451-3365
www.ccrose.org

East Bay Rose Society
East San Francisco Bay
510-537-0443
www.eastbayroses.org/

Gold Country Rose Society
Auburn–Grass Valley
530-885-8230
www.geocities.com/
RainForest/wetlands/1395

Golden Gate Rose Society
Peninsula Area
415-474-3714
www.ggrs.org

Golden Sierra Rose Society
Columbia Area
209-536-9415

Humboldt Rose Society
Fortuna–Eureka
707-822-9678

Lake County Rose Society
Lake County
707-263-8249

Lodi–Woodbridge Rose
Society
Lodi–Woodbridge
209-729-3954

Marin Rose Society
Marin County
415-388-8552
www.marinrose.org/

Mendocino Rose Society
Mendocino
707-459-8625

Monterey Bay Rose Society
Monterey Bay Area
831-786-0955
www.montereyrosesociety.
org/

Mother Lode Rose Society
Amador County
209-245-3754
www.motherloderose.org/

Mount Diablo Rose Society
Pleasanton–Livermore–Dub
lin–San Ramon–Castro
Valley
925-829-4929

North Bay Rose Society
Vallejo–Fairfield–Benicia
707-745-5898

Peninsula Rose Society
SanBruno–Menlo–Park–
Redwood City
650-323-5268

Redwood Empire Rose
Society
Napa–Santa Rosa
707-542-7661
www.geocities.com/
rose_society

Sacramento Rose Society
Sacramento Area
916-487-9444
www.sactorose.org/

San Francisco Rose Society
San Francisco
415-661-4619
www.geocities.com/
PicketFence/3705/

San Joaquin Valley Rose
Society
Fresno Area
559-229-7329
www.geocities.com/Rain
Forest/2548

San Mateo County Rose
Society
San Mateo County
650-372-0516

Santa Clara County Rose
Society
San Jose
408-293-5073
http://mejac.palo-
alto.ca.us/orgs/sccrs/

Shasta Rose Society
Redding
530-547-3605
www.shastarosesociety.org/

Sierra Foothills Rose
Society
Sacramento–Placer–El
Dorado Counties
530-626-1722
www.sactorose.org/

Stockton Rose Society
Stockton Area
209-938-4362

Woodland Library Rose
Club
Woodland
530-662-4020

Garden Centers and Suppliers

www.helpmefind.com/
roses lists over 85 rose
suppliers, growers, whole-
salers and retailers
throughout California

Vintage Gardens
2833 Old Gravenstein
Highway So.
Sebastopol, CA 95472
707-829-2035
www.vintagegardens.com
gita@vintagegardens.com

Amity Heritage Roses
PO Box 357
Hydesville, CA 95547
707-768-2040
www.amityheritagesroses.
com
TandJ@AmityHeritageRose.
com

Mendocino Heirloom Roses
PO Box 904
Redwood Valley, CA 95470
707-485-6219
www.heritageroses.com
smontoya@pacific.net

Arena Roses
1041 Paso Robles Street
Paso Robles, CA 93446
888-466-7434 or
805-238-3742
www.arenaroses.com

Regan Nursery
4268 Decoto Road
Fremont, CA 94558
510-797-3222 or
800-249-4680
www.regannursery.com

Garden Valley Ranch
498 Pepper Road
Petaluma, CA 94952
707-795-0919
www.gardenvalley.com
info@gardenvalley.com

Moore's Miniature Roses
2519 East Noble
Visalia, CA 93292
www.miniaturerose.com
sequoianursery@miniature
roses.com

Rose Acres
6641 Crystal Blvd.
El Dorado, CA 95623
530-626-1722

Soil Testing

Bolsa Analytical
Laboratories
2337 Technology Parkway,
Suite K
Hollister, CA 95023
831-637-4590

Caltest Analytical
Laboratory
1884 North Kelly Road
Napa, CA 94558
707-258-4000
www.caltestlab.com
caltest@caltestlab.com

Cerco Analytical, Inc.
3942-A Valley Avenue,
Suite A
Pleasanton, CA 94566-4715
925-462-2771

Chromalab, Inc.
1220 Quarry Lane
Pleasanton, CA 94566
925-484-1919
www.chromalab.com

Environmental
Technological Services
1343 Redwood Way
Petaluma, CA 94954
707-795-9605

Perry Laboratory
471 Airport Boulevard
Watsonville, CA 95076
831-722-7606

Plant Sciences
342 Green Valley Road
Watsonville, CA 95076
408-728-7771
www.plantsciences.com

Scientific Environmental
Laboratories, Inc.
924 Industrial Avenue
Palo Alto, CA 94303
650-856-6011

Sequoia Analytical
1455 McDowell Boulevard,
Suite N
Petaluma, CA 94594
707-792-1865
www.sequoialabs.com

Signet Testing Laboratories,
Inc.
3121 Diablo Avenue
Hayward, CA 94545
510-887-8484

Soil and Plant Laboratory
352 Mathew Street
Santa Clara, CA 95052
408-727-0330
www.soilandplant
laboratory.com
splab7@earthlink.net

Soil Control Laboratory
42 Hangar Way
Watsonville, CA 95075
831-724-5422

Websites

www.bridgesroses.com
www.edmundsroses.com
www.everyrose.com
www.heirloomroses.com
www.helpmefind.com/roses
www.jacksonandperkins.com
www.rdrop.com/~paul/
www.rosarian.com
www.rose.org
www.rosegathering.com
www.rosemagazine.com
www.weeksroses.com

Reference Books

Botanica's Pocket Roses. 2001. Foreword by William A. Grant. Whitecap Books, Vancouver/Toronto.

Brown, Deni. 1996. *Eyewitness Garden Handbook: Roses.* DK Publishing, New York.

Druitt, Liz. 1996. *The Organic Rose Garden.* Taylor Publishing Co., Dallas.

Krüssmann, Gerd. 1981. *The Complete Book of Roses.* Timber Press, Portland.

MacOboy, Stirling. 1993. *The Ultimate Rose Book.* Henry N. Abrams Inc., New York.

Modern Roses XI: *The World Encyclopedia of Roses.* 2000. Academic Press, London/San Diego.

Moody, Mary. 1992. *The Illustrated Encyclopedia of Roses.* Timber Press, Portland.

Phillips, Roger and Rix, Martyn. 1988. *The Random House Book of Roses.* Random House. New York.

Reddell, Rayford Clayton. 1998. *The Rose Bible.* Chronicle Books, San Francisco.

Sammis, Kathy. 1995. *The American Garden Guides: Rose Gardening.* Pantheon Books, New York.

Taylor's Guide to Roses. Revised Edition. 1995. Houghton Mifflin Co, Boston/New York.

Walheim and The Editors of the National Gardening Association. 2000. *Roses for Dummies, 2nd Edition.* IDG Books Worldwide, Inc., Foster City, California.

Glossary

acid soil: soil with a pH lower than 7.0

alkaline soil: soil with a pH higher than 7.0

bud union: the junction on a stem where a bud of one plant has been grafted to the stock of another

button eye (button center): the round center in a double rose blossom, composed of stamens that have turned into petals; these petals are tightly packed and cannot unfold, which gives the flower a button-like appearance

calyx: the outer whorl of a flower, usually consisting of green, leafy sepals

cane: a woody, often flexible stem, usually arising from the base of the plant

cultivar: a *culti*vated (bred) plant *vari*ety with one or more distinct differences from the parent species, e.g., in flower color or disease resistance

deadhead: to remove spent flowers to maintain a neat appearance and encourage a longer blooming period

desiccation: loss of moisture through foliage

double flower: a flower with an unusually large number of petals, often caused by mutation of the stamens into petals

forma (f.): a naturally occurring variant that retains most characteristics of the species but differs naturally in some way, such as plant size or leaf color; below the level of variety in biological classification

genus: category of biological classification between the species and family levels; e.g., the genus *Rosa*

grafting: method of propagating a tree or shrub by joining a bud or cutting of a desired plant with the rootstock of another plant; the tissues grow together and top growth develops in the form of the more desirable plant

hardpan: a layer of compacted subsoil that often prevents the penetration of water or of shrub or tree roots. Hardpan can occur naturally or be caused by repeated cultivation by mechanical means

hardy: capable of surviving unfavorable conditions, such as cold weather

hip: the often colorful fruit of a rose, containing the seeds

hybrid: a plant resulting from cross-breeding between varieties, species or genera; the hybrid will not breed true (yield identical offspring) when crossed with itself

inflorescence: a shoot bearing more than one flower and usually clusters of flowers

lateral (lateral bud): bud produced in the junction between the stem and a leaf

muddled: a flower with petals that are disorganized, not forming a pattern

neutral soil: soil with a pH of 7.0

pH: a measure of acidity or alkalinity (the lower the pH, the higher the acidity); the pH of soil influences availability of nutrients for plants

pesticide: a general term for any compound used to kill insects, mites, weeds, fungi, bacteria or other pests

pith: the spongy central tissue of a stem

quilled: the narrow, tubular shape of petals or florets of some flowers

remontant: able to bloom again one or more times during a growing season

rhizome: a root-like stem that grows horizontally underground and from which shoots and true roots emerge

rootball: the root mass and surrounding soil of a container-grown plant or a plant dug out of the ground

rootstock: the root system and lower portion of a woody plant (the stock) onto which another plant can be grafted; a vertical rhizome

rosetting: distorted leaf growth caused by viral damage. The leaves or side branches grow close together in the form of a rosette

runner: a modified, creeping stem that runs along the ground, forming roots and new shoots at the joints or tip

self-seeding: reproducing by means of seeds without human assistance, so that new plants constantly replace those that die

semi-double flower: a flower with petals in two or three rings

semi-hardy: a plant capable of surviving the climatic conditions of a given region if protected

sepals: leaf-like structures that protect the flower bud and surround the petals in the opened flower

single flower: a flower with a single ring of petals

species: the original plant from which cultivars are derived; the fundamental unit of biological classification, indicated by a two-part scientific name, e.g., *Rosa glauca* (*glauca* is the specific epithet)

sport: an atypical plant or flower that arises through mutation; some sports are horticulturally desirable and propagated as new cultivars

subspecies (subsp.): a naturally occurring, regional form of a species, often isolated from other subspecies but still potentially interfertile with them

sucker: a cane that sprouts from the roots or from below the bud union, therefore originating from the rootstock and different from the grafted plant

tender: incapable of surviving the climatic conditions of a given region; requiring protection from frost or cold

terminal bud: a bud formed at the tip of a stem or branch

variety (var.): a naturally occurring variant of a species; below the level of subspecies in biological classification

Index

A

Abraham. *See* Abraham Darby
Abraham Darby, 122
Alba Meidiland. *See* White Meidiland
Albertine, 160
Altissimo, 161
Altus. *See* Altissimo
Amber Queen, 212
America, 162
American Pillar, 163
Andeli. *See* Double Delight
Aotearoa. *See* New Zealand
Aotearoa-New Zealand. *See* New Zealand
Apricot Parfait. *See* Evelyn
Aroyqueli. *See* Gold Medal

B

Baby Blanket, 150
Ballerina, 123
Barbra Streisand, 182
Beke. *See* Peace
Belle of Portugal, 164
Belle Portugaise. *See* Belle of Portugal
Berkeley. *See* Tournament of Roses
Betty Boop, 213
Bizarre Triomphant. *See* Charles de Mills
Blanc de Coubert. *See* Blanc Double de Coubert
Blanc Double de Coubert, 124
Blanche Double de Coubert. *See* Blanc Double de Coubert
Blanc Meillandecor. *See* White Meidiland
Blaze Improved, 165
Blaze Superior. *See* Blaze Improved
Blooming Carpet. *See* Flower Carpet

Blueberry Hill, 214
Bonica, 125
Bonica '82. *See* Bonica
Bonica Meidiland. *See* Bonica
Bride's Dream, 183
Buff Beauty, 126
Butterfly Rose. *See* Mutabilis

C

C.W.S. *See* Canadian White Star
Cadillac DeVille. *See* Moonstone
Cal Trans. *See* Gizmo
Carefree Wonder, 127
Carefully Wonder. *See* Carefree Wonder
Centenary of Federation. *See* Betty Boop
Chantoli. *See* Sunset Celebration
Charles de Mills, 106
Charles Mills. *See* Charles de Mills
Charles Wills. *See* Charles de Mills
Cheerio. *See* Playboy
Cherry Parfait, 234
Chilterns. *See* Red Ribbons
China Doll, 128
City of Newcastle Bicentennary. *See* Veteran's Honor
Climbing Cécile Brünner, 166
Climbing Don Juan. *See* Don Juan
Climbing Flutterbye. *See* Flutterbye
Climbing Mignon. *See* Climbing Cécile Brünner
Climbing Mme. Cécile Brünner. *See* Climbing Cécile Brünner
Climbing Sweetheart Rose. *See* Climbing Cécile Brünner
Colonial White. *See* Sombreuil
Country Abraham. *See* Abraham Darby

Country Lass. *See* Baby Blanket
County Abraham. *See* Abraham Darby
Crazy for You. *See* Fourth of July
Creepy. *See* Ralph's Creeper
Crystalline, 184
Cupcake, 242

D

Dainty Bess, 185
Demokracie. *See* Blaze Improved
Demon. *See* Bonica
Diana, Princess of Wales, 186
Don Juan, 167
Dortmund, 168
Double Delight, 187
Dr. Wolfgang Pöschl. *See* Canadian White Star
Dublin Bay, 169
Duchesse d'Istrie. *See* William Lobb
Dynastie. *See* Carefree Wonder

E

Easy Going, 215
Eglantine. See *Rosa eglanteria*
Electron, 188
Elina, 189
Elizabeth Taylor, 190
Emera. *See* Flower Carpet
Emera Pavement. *See* Flower Carpet
Emeura. *See* Flower Carpet
English Yellow. *See* Graham Thomas
Europeana, 216
Evelyn, 129
Exotic. *See* Sunset Celebration
Everblooming Dr. W. Van Fleet. *See* New Dawn

F

Fairhope, 243
Fairy. *See* The Fairy
Fairytale Queen. *See* Bride's Dream

Fantin-Latour, 107
Fée des Neiges. *See* Iceberg
Feerie. *See* The Fairy
Felicia, 130
Félicité. *See* Félicité Parmentier
Félicité Parmentier, 108
Fellowship. *See* Livin' Easy
Ferdi. *See* Ferdy
Ferdy, 151
Fiery Sunsation. *See* Red Ribbons
Five Roses Rose. *See* Veteran's Honor
Floral Carpet. *See* Flower Carpet
Flower Carpet, 152
Flutterbye, 170
Fourth of July, 171
Fragrant Cloud, 191
Frau Dagmar Hartopp. *See* Frau Dagmar Hastrup
Frau Dagmar Hastrup, 131
Fredrosen. *See* Peace
French Lace, 217
Friesia. *See* Sunsprite

G

Gemini, 192
Gift of Life, 193
Giggles, 244
Gioia. *See* Peace
Gizmo, 245
Gloria Dei. *See* Peace
Glossy Rose. See *Rosa virginiana*
Glowing Amber, 246
Glowing Carpet. *See* Ralph's Creeper
Gold Medal, 235
Golden Celebration, 132
Golden Showers, 172
Golden Sunblaze. *See* Rise 'n' Shine
Golden Wings, 133
Gourmet Popcorn, 247
Graham Stuart Thomas. *See* Graham Thomas
Graham Thomas, 134
Green Ice, 248

Gul e Rescht. *See* Rose de Rescht

H

Hanabi. *See* Fourth of July
Haendel. *See* Handel
Händel. *See* Handel
Handel, 173
Hannah Gordon. *See* Nicole
Hansa, 135
Hansen's. *See* Hansa
Harisonii. *See* Harison's Yellow
Harison's Yellow, 109
Heckenzauber. *See* Sexy Rexy
Heideröslein Nozomi. *See* Nozomi
Heidetraum. *See* Flower Carpet
Heritage, 136
Highveld Sun. *See* Ralph's Creeper
Hot Cocoa, 218
Hot Tamale, 249

I

Iceberg, 219
Imperial Blaze. *See* Blaze Improved
Incognito, 250
Irresistible, 251
Island Fire. *See* Red Ribbons

J

Jacques Cartier, 110
Jean Kenneally, 252
Just Joey, 195

L

Lady of the Dawn, 220
Lady in Red. *See* Veteran's Honor
Lavaglow. *See* Lavaglut
Lavaglut, 221
Lavender Lassie, 137
Liebeszauber, 196
Limelight. *See* St. Patrick

Linda Campbell, 138
Livin' Easy, 222
Louise Odier, 111
Love, 236

M

Madame Alfred Carrière, 174
Madame Hardy, 112
Macha. *See* Handel
Magic Carousel. *See* Magic Carrousel
Magic Carrousel, 253
Mainaufeuer. *See* Red Ribbons
Märchenkönigin. *See* Bride's Dream
Marchesa Boccella. *See* Jacques Cartier
Marilyn Monroe, 197
Marquise Boçella. *See* Jacques Cartier
Marquise Boccella. *See* Jacques Cartier
Mary Rose, 139
Mayflower. *See* The Mayflower
Meidomonac. *See* Bonica
Mellow Yellow, 198
Melody Parfumée, 237
Memorial Day, 199
Minnie Pearl, 254
Miss Flippins, 255
Mister Lincoln, 200
Mlle. Cécile Brünner. *See* Climbing
     Cécile Brünner
Mlle. de Sombreuil. *See* Sombreuil
Mme. A. Meilland. *See* Peace
Mme. de Stella. *See* Louise Odier
Mr. A. Lincoln. *See* Mister Lincoln
Mr. Lincoln. *See* Mister Lincoln
Moonstone, 201
Mullard Jubilee. *See* Electron
Mutabilis, 113

N

New Blaze. *See* Blaze Improved
New Dawn, 175
New Zealand, 202
Nicole, 223

Nozomi, 153
Nuage Parfumé. *See* Fragrant Cloud

O

Oxfordshire. *See* Baby Blanket
Outta the Blue, 140
Old Velvet Moss. *See* William Lobb

P

Pat Austin, 141
Peace, 203
Peaudouce. *See* Elina
Pierrine, 256
Pink Flower Carpet. *See* Flower
    Carpet
Pink Simplicity. *See* Simplicity
Pioneer Rose. *See* Harison's Yellow
Playboy, 224
Poesie. *See* Tournament of Roses
Poetry in Motion. *See* Gift of Life
Prinz Eugen von Savoyen. *See* Amber
    Queen
Pristine, 204
Prospero, 142
Purple Heart, 225

Q

Queen Elizabeth, 238
Queen of England. *See* Queen
    Elizabeth
Queen of the Violets. *See* Reine des
    Violettes

R

Rainbow's End, 257
Ralph's Creeper, 154
Raspberry Ice. *See* Nicole
Red Ribbons, 155
Red-leafed Rose. See *Rosa glauca*
Reine des Violettes, 114

Rise 'n' Shine, 258
Roberta. *See* Heritage
Rose De Rescht. *See* Rose de Rescht
Rosa
    banksiae lutea, 98
    banksiae lutea plena. See *Rosa
        banksiae lutea*
    chinensis mutabilis. See Mutabilis
        eglanteria, 99
    ferruginea. See *Rosa glauca*
    foetida harisonii. See Harison's
        Yellow
    glauca, 100
    lutea hoggii. See Harison's Yellow
    odorata 'Mutabilis.' See Mutabilis
    rubiginosa. See *Rosa eglanteria*
    rubrifolia. See *Rosa glauca*
    suavifolia. See *Rosa eglanteria*
    virginiana, 101
    walpoleana. See *Rosa eglanteria*
    x *harisonii. See* Harison's Yellow
    x *harisonii* 'Harison's Yellow.'
        See Harison's Yellow
    x *harisonii* 'Yellow Rose of Texas.'
        See Harison's Yellow
Rosarium Uetersen, 176
Rose de Rescht, 115
Royal Sunset, 177

S

Saint Patrick. *See* St. Patrick
Sally Holmes, 143
Scentimental, 226
Schneewittchen. *See* Iceberg
Sea Foam, 156
Seafoam. *See* Sea Foam
Seminole Wind. *See* Rosarium
    Uetersen
Sexy Rexy, 227
Shakespeare's Rose.
    See *Rosa eglanteria*
Shakespeare's Eglantine.
    See *Rosa eglanteria*

Sheila's Perfume, 228
Simplicity, 229
Snow Bride, 259
Snowbride. *See* Snow Bride
Sombreuil, 178
Sommermorgen. *See* Baby Blanket
St. Patrick, 205
Stainless Steel, 206
Stanwell Perpetual, 116
Starina, 260
Sublimely Single. *See* Altissimo
Summer Morning. *See* Baby Blanket
Sunbird. *See* Hot Tamale
Sunset Celebration, 207
Sunsprite, 230
Sweet Briar Rose. See *Rosa eglanteria*

T

Tabris. *See* Nicole
Tall Poppy. *See* Linda Campbell
Tamora, 144
The Artistic Rose. *See* Dainty Bess
The Fairy, 145
The Mayflower, 146
The Mayflower Rose. *See* The
  Mayflower
The New Dawn. *See* New Dawn
The Queen Elizabeth Rose. *See* Queen
  Elizabeth
The Work Continues. *See* Diana,
  Princess of Wales
Theresa Bugnet. *See* Thérèse Bugnet
Thérèse Bugnet, 147
Tipo Idéale. *See* Mutabilis
Tournament of Roses, 239
Trailing Red. *See* Ralph's Creeper
Trumpeter, 231

U

Uetersen. *See* Rosarium Uetersen

V

Valerie Swane. *See* Crystalline
Veteran's Honor, 208
Violette Parfumée. *See* Melody
  Parfumée
Virginiana Rose. See *Rosa virginiana*

W

Warm Wishes. *See* Sunset Celebration
Westerland, 179
Whisper, 209
White Meidiland, 157
William Lobb, 117
Winsome, 261

Y

Yellow Lady Banks Rose. See *Rosa
  banksiae lutea*